Beyond Air–Sea Battle: The Debate Over US Military Strategy in Asia

Aaron L. Friedberg

Beyond Air–Sea Battle: The Debate Over US Military Strategy in Asia

Aaron L. Friedberg

IISS The International Institute for Strategic Studies

The International Institute for Strategic Studies

Arundel House | 13–15 Arundel Street | Temple Place | London | WC2R 3DX | UK

First published April 2014 by **Routledge**
4 Park Square, Milton Park, Abingdon, Oxon, OX14 4RN

for **The International Institute for Strategic Studies**
Arundel House, 13–15 Arundel Street, Temple Place, London, WC2R 3DX, UK
www.iiss.org

Simultaneously published in the USA and Canada by **Routledge**
711 Third Avenue, New York, NY, 10017, USA

Routledge is an imprint of Taylor & Francis, an Informa Business

DIRECTOR-GENERAL AND CHIEF EXECUTIVE Dr John Chipman
EDITOR Dr Nicholas Redman
ASSISTANT EDITOR Mona Moussavi
EDITORIAL Chris Raggett, Zoe Rutherford
COVER/PRODUCTION John Buck, Kelly Verity
COVER IMAGES Air Power Australia; Xinhua; Cpl. Ken Kalemkarian/USMC

The International Institute for Strategic Studies is an independent centre for research, information and debate on the problems of conflict, however caused, that have, or potentially have, an important military content. The Council and Staff of the Institute are international and its membership is drawn from almost 100 countries. The Institute is independent and it alone decides what activities to conduct. It owes no allegiance to any government, any group of governments or any political or other organisation. The IISS stresses rigorous research with a forward-looking policy orientation and places particular emphasis on bringing new perspectives to the strategic debate.

The Institute's publications are designed to meet the needs of a wider audience than its own membership and are available on subscription, by mail order and in good bookshops. Further details at www.iiss.org.

British Library Cataloguing in Publication Data
A catalogue record for this book is available from the British Library

Library of Congress Cataloging in Publication Data

ADELPHI series
ISSN 1944-5571

ADELPHI 444
ISBN 978-1-138-80832-4

Contents

ACKNOWLEDGEMENTS

I would like to thank Jackie Newmyer Deal, Daniel DeMots, David Epstein, James FitzSimonds, Kurt Guthe, Thomas Mahnken, Dale Rielage, Nadège Rolland, Stephen Rosen, Gabriel Schoenfeld, Mark Stokes and Jan van Tol for their helpful comments and suggestions. A grant from the Smith Richardson Foundation enabled me to complete the research for, and writing of, this book. I am grateful to the American Academy for Strategic Education for providing institutional support. Thanks also to Nick Redman and Adam Ward of the International Institute for Strategic Studies for their interest in this project, and to Mona Moussavi for editing the manuscript.

GLOSSARY

A2/AD	anti-access/area denial
Air-breathing/non-air-breathing platform	Propulsion systems that do/do not rely on external oxygen drawn into the engine through inlets to maintain combustion.
AMS	Academy of Military Sciences
ASAT	anti-satellite
ASB	Air–Sea Battle
ASBM	anti-ship ballistic missile
ASBO	Air–Sea Battle Office
ASCEL	Active Strategic Counterattacks on Exterior Lines
ASCM	anti-ship cruise missile
ASW	anti-submarine warfare
BMD	ballistic-missile defence
C3I	command, control, communications and intelligence
C4ISR	command, control, communications, computers, intelligence, surveillance and reconnaissance
CCD	camouflage, concealment and deception
CCP	Chinese Communist Party
CM	cruise missile
DE	directed energy. A directed-energy weapon is one in which focused electromagnetic energy or particles are used for lethal or non-lethal effect.
Direct-ascent system	Anti-satellite projectiles designed to fly to their target on a straight or parabolic path.
EW	electronic warfare
Hardening	Designing or modifying structures to resist conventional and/or nuclear attack.
IAD	integrated air defence
ICBM	intercontinental ballistic missile
INF Treaty	Intermediate-Range Nuclear Forces Treaty
ISR	intelligence, surveillance and reconnaissance
JASSM	Joint Air-to-Surface Standoff Missile
JOAC	Joint Operational Access Concept

Kinetic-kill weapon	A weapon designed to destroy its target through direct physical impact.
LCS	Littoral Combat Ship
MRBM	medium-range ballistic missile
OTH	over-the-horizon radar. A radar capable of tracking targets at very long ranges, reliant on atmospheric effects to attain range.
OPSEC	operational security
PGM	precision-guided munition
PRC	People's Republic of China
PLA	People's Liberation Army
PLAAF	People's Liberation Army Air Force
PLAN	People's Liberation Army Navy
QDR	Quadrennial Defense Review
RSC	reconnaissance–strike complex. A Soviet concept describing the combination of precision-guided weapons, sensors and automated command-and-control subsystems.
THAAD	Terminal High Altitude Area Defense
UAV	unmanned aerial vehicle
UCAS	unmanned combat air system
UGF	underground facility
UUV	unmanned underwater vehicle

For N

INTRODUCTION

In Asia, as elsewhere in the world, the strategic position of the United States rests ultimately on its ability to project power over great distances. This unique capacity enables the US to extend security guarantees to its allies, who in turn provide it with local bases and facilities. Despite ongoing improvements in the technologies of communication and transportation, these remain essential to the task of sustaining US forces thousands of miles from home. The ability of the US to project military power and its global alliance system are thus mutually reinforcing.

For a time, following the collapse of the Soviet Union, US power-projection capabilities were essentially unchallenged. American decision-makers could deploy and operate their air and naval units at will virtually anywhere in the world, including along the eastern periphery of Eurasia. Despite post-Cold War cutbacks, the US nuclear arsenal remained vast and continued to provide a credible backstop to its forward-deployed conventional forces. Washington was thus well situated to deter or defeat attacks or attempts at coercion directed at its local friends and allies, to defend vital sea lanes and, if necessary, to bring coercive pressure of its own to bear on potentially hostile powers.

American superiority was on display during 1995–96 when, following Chinese missile tests aimed at influencing the results of Taiwan's first free presidential elections, the Clinton administration dispatched two carrier battle groups to waters off the island. In retrospect, this incident appears to have marked an inflection point in China's military development and in the Sino-American strategic relationship. At the time, it seemed painfully obvious that the People's Liberation Army (PLA) had no viable options to offer in response. In the aftermath of the crisis, however, Beijing began to ramp up military spending and, in particular, its investments in capabilities designed to deter, slow and, perhaps eventually, defeat US attempts to project power into and across the Western Pacific. While these actions were motivated in the first instance by the desire to find solutions to a pressing operational problem, from the start, they had the potential to produce major strategic shifts. If China could counter the United States' conventional power-projection capabilities and neutralise its extended nuclear deterrent, it might some day be able to replace the US as the preponderant player in the region.

Nearly two decades on, Beijing's investments have begun to bear fruit. China's ongoing military build-up, and especially the expansion of its long-range nuclear forces and its development of so-called 'anti-access/area-denial' (A2/AD) capabilities, poses a serious and growing threat to the American position in East Asia, and to the security of other regional powers. Because they challenge Washington's ability, and perhaps its willingness, to project power in the region, the continuing growth of these forces could call American security guarantees into question, weakening the alliances on which they rest and eventually undermining the United States' place as the preponderant

Asia-Pacific power. Left unchecked, perceived shifts in the regional military balance away from the US and its allies, and towards China, could also raise the risks of miscalculation and deterrence failure.

Although the essential nature of this challenge has been evident since the latter part of the 1990s, for a variety of reasons the US armed forces, the Department of Defense and the government as a whole have been slow to formulate a coherent response. Substantial residual advantages in many areas of military capability, combined with an initial under-estimation of the extent, seriousness and significance of the People's Republic of China's (PRC) build-up, made this task seem less pressing for a time. High-impact, unanticipated events have twice conspired to deflect attention and resources from the problem. If not for the 9/11 terror attacks (and the two major wars that followed in their wake) and the 2008 financial crisis, the US would no doubt have made further progress in responding to China's initiatives than it has today. Last but not least, the unusual, mixed character of the Sino-American relationship, and the hope that it will evolve naturally towards ever-higher levels of stability and cooperation, has also helped to mitigate Washington's competitive reflexes.

Despite all this, in the last few years, the continuing momentum of China's development and procurement programmes, its growing assertiveness towards its neighbours and the likelihood of persistent downward pressures on US defence spending have combined to concentrate the minds of American strategists. After a decade of emphasising counter-insurgency and counter-terrorism operations, finding a credible response to China's A2/AD capabilities has emerged as the central task confronting military planners, and it is likely to remain so for some time to come. Addressing this problem would not have been easy in any event, and tight fiscal constraints will make it even more difficult, but doing so has become an urgent necessity.

Much is at stake in the current debate over the future of US military strategy in Asia. A fully thought-through and articulated strategy is essential if decision-makers are to rationally reshape the plans and programmes of the armed services in an era of stringency and – equally important – win the domestic support necessary to fund them. A serious, sustained effort to slow the increasingly evident erosion in the regional balance of power is needed to give substance to recent talk of a 'pivot' towards Asia and to help persuade the United States' regional allies to step up their own contributions to this collective undertaking. Finally, while there are no guarantees, a credible strategy and a force posture to back it up provide the best hope of deterring aggression and keeping the peace.

CHAPTER ONE

An emerging challenge

The Chinese military capabilities that today represent an increasing threat to the US position in East Asia are themselves a response to a danger that People's Liberation Army (PLA) planners first began to perceive as emanating from the United States over two decades ago. In fact, the chain of causality can be traced even further back. The high-tech weapons and concepts of operation that caused Chinese analysts such anxiety in the early 1990s started to develop in the late 1970s, as NATO planners searched for ways to counter the massive ground and air forces being assembled in Central Europe by the Warsaw Pact. Three decades later, and after an interval during which it seemed that American military superiority might never again be challenged, the wheel has come full circle.

Origins

The seeds of the challenge now emerging for the US were sown during the 1990s. This was a period punctuated by a series of sometimes overlapping shocks and crises that galvanised China's political leaders, focused the attention of its strategic planners, freed up resources and yielded a broad consensus on how best to apply them in building the nation's military power.

The end of the Cold War

The collapse of the Soviet Union had contradictory implications for Chinese security, all but eliminating one threat while simultaneously amplifying another.

Since the mid-1960s, the two communist giants had been locked in a tense and bitter stand-off. Despite this, in the mid-1980s, Chinese strategists concluded that the re-establishment of a rough balance of power between the US and Soviet blocs meant that the threat of war was receding. The prevailing trends in the world therefore favoured 'peace and development'. This assessment, in turn, justified a full embrace of Deng Xiaoping's economic policies of 'reform and opening up', and set the stage for a preliminary revision in military doctrine. Instead of gearing up for a titanic struggle for survival between huge land armies backed by nuclear weapons (a 'people's war under modern conditions'), the PLA would henceforth focus on preparing for 'limited, local wars'. Such conflicts would be constrained in duration, aims and geographic scope, and they would most likely be waged using only conventional weapons.[1]

The demise of the Soviet Union validated these judgements but also raised the spectre of a new strategic rivalry with the US. For two decades, Washington and Beijing had been drawn together by a shared fear of perceived growing Soviet power; now the threat was gone, and with it went the strongest rationale for a continued strategic alignment. To make matters worse, Chinese strategists were convinced that, having dispensed with the Soviet Union, Washington would turn its attention to undermining the last remaining bastion of the 'socialist way'. During the Cold War, the existence of another superpower had forced the US to act with a measure of restraint; now it would be free to indulge in its hegemonic and interventionist tendencies.[2]

The First Gulf War

The decisive American defeat of Saddam Hussein's army in 1991 confirmed Beijing's worst fears and added a new dimension to its anxieties. In the new world order, Washington could mobilise widespread international support and even win the endorsement of the United Nations for its adventures. If the US could violate the sovereignty and brush aside the resistance of a major power in the Middle East, there was a danger that it could do the same in other parts of the world.

In addition to providing an impressive demonstration of the United States' newfound influence and resolve, the First Gulf War highlighted the vast and growing gap between the capabilities of its armed forces and those of virtually every other nation. That Iraqi forces had widely been regarded as formidable before the start of hostilities, and used many of the same weapons and tactics as the PLA, did not go unnoticed in Beijing. In the war's aftermath, Chinese strategists began an extended period of intensive analysis and remarkably candid self-criticism, with some themes clear from the outset. The war demonstrated that new technologies would play a decisive role in future conflicts. China now needed to prepare not only for 'limited, local wars', but also for 'local wars under high-technology conditions'.[3] Thanks to its pioneering role, the US enjoyed a huge lead in virtually every relevant area of capability, and seemed poised to advance even further by exploiting the potential of a new 'revolution in military affairs'. China needed to catch up but, in the meantime, PLA planners had to devise means of offsetting and countering the United States' advantages, enabling the 'weak to defeat the strong'.[4]

The 1995–96 Taiwan Strait Crisis

In March 1996, after several months of growing tensions, China test-fired unarmed ballistic missiles into the waters off Taiwan. This unprecedented display was aimed both at Taipei, which was seen in Beijing as drifting dangerously towards independence, and at Washington, which appeared to be aiding and abetting Taiwan. The Clinton administration responded to this show of force with one of its own, deploying two aircraft-carrier battle groups to the vicinity of the island.[5]

These events were followed by a ratcheting down of tensions and at least a superficial improvement in Sino-American relations, but they left a lasting sense of apprehension and mistrust. It was only in their aftermath that US intelligence analysts and defence planners began to take seriously the possibility of a future war with the People's Republic of China (PRC).[6] While Chinese strategists did not need any encouragement in this regard, the crisis gave an added measure of specificity and intensity to their deliberations. As David Shambaugh explains, 'PLA leaders had long wondered whether they would have to confront the vaunted US military in a Taiwan crisis – now they could assume so.'[7]

Rather than a general emphasis on modernising in all dimensions at once, the prospect of American intervention with carrier-based aircraft gave planners a very specific set of problems on which to focus. Equally important, top military leaders now had a concrete threat on which to base their requests for more resources.

Following the 1989 Tiananmen Square incident, during which the army's loyalty had arguably saved the regime, the crisis of 1995–96 further strengthened the PLA's hand in dealing with its civilian masters.[8] It also had an impact on decisions about weapons procurement and research. In 1996, the People's Liberation Army Navy (PLAN) purchased four

Russian-built *Sovremenny* destroyers equipped with the Raduga 3M80 *Moskit* (NATO codename: SS-N-22 *Sunburn*) supersonic, anti-ship cruise missiles. The missiles had been designed in the Soviet era as a counter to US aircraft carriers and their escorts.[9] Preliminary studies of a possible land-based anti-ship ballistic missile were also begun shortly after the Taiwan Strait Crisis.[10]

Kosovo

If the First Gulf War revealed the potentially devastating impact of the United States' technological edge, and the Taiwan crisis highlighted its apparent proclivity for intervention, the 1999 war over Kosovo reinforced both concerns.

This time, Washington did not go to the UN for approval, instead rounding up a few of its NATO allies to provide a cloak of international legitimacy. In the First Gulf War, the Americans could at least justify their actions by pointing out that Iraq had invaded another sovereign state; in Kosovo, they were openly supporting what could only be regarded as a separatist movement. Given Beijing's fear of 'splittists' in Tibet and Xinjiang, to say nothing of Taiwan, this was a chilling new departure.

Eight years after Iraq, the US military had made further strides in capability. In addition to satellites, the Americans made extensive use of command-and-control aircraft equipped with radars that could locate and track mobile targets on the ground. The newly operational, stealthy B-2 bomber flew round-trip missions from bases in the continental US, destroying command-and-control and air-defence systems, and clearing the way for strikes by other manned aircraft. A much higher percentage of the weapons delivered against targets in Serbia were 'smart', precision-guided munitions, as opposed to 'dumb', unguided bombs.[11] Most impressive of all, the US-led coalition achieved its strategic objectives primarily through the use of air power, without suffering a single casualty.

Ironically, it was the precision of most allied air operations that made it virtually impossible to convince Beijing that a misguided strike on its embassy in Belgrade was an accident.[12] Startled by what they perceived as a new level of American aggression, some Chinese analysts began to question whether peace and development were truly the prevailing trends in world affairs. If this was no longer the case, war might actually be imminent and defence preparations would have to be given priority over other national objectives. Although cooler heads eventually prevailed, David Finkelstein concludes that the Kosovo conflict 'convinced those who were previously skeptical about US willingness to intervene militarily in a Taiwan scenario that they were probably wrong', and served as a justification for further increases in defence spending.[13] Much as the 1995–96 crisis had encouraged a search for ways to attack aircraft carriers, so too the war in Serbia caused PLA planners to highlight the importance of mastering specific military tasks, including the so-called 'three attacks and three defences': countering enemy helicopters, and stealthy aircraft and cruise missiles; and defending against precision air-strikes, electronic warfare (EW) and space-based reconnaissance.[14]

Concept

The events of 1995–96 and 1999 gave additional impetus and direction to the debate that had begun in 1991 over the changing nature of war and the future of Chinese strategy. Although this discussion continues today, with no full agreement on some important issues,[15] by the end of the 1990s, PLA theorists and planners had reached a broad consensus on the character of the challenge they faced and the basic principles that should guide their response.

The US appeared to be in the process of developing what Soviet military theorists had since the early 1980s labelled a 'reconnaissance–strike complex' (RSC). In order to defeat it, the PLA would have to build one of its own, albeit with distinctive 'Chinese characteristics'. As the label suggests, an RSC is a 'system-of-systems' designed to locate an enemy's forces, weapons and facilities, and to disable or destroy them using a mix of non-kinetic weapons (including EW and computer-network attacks) and precision-guided conventional munitions. In the Gulf, and again over Serbia, for example, the US had employed satellites, command-and-control aircraft and unmanned aerial vehicles (UAVs). These were used to locate, identify and support the targeting of everything from electric power plants and underground bunkers to camouflaged gun emplacements and moving vehicles. After using jamming and stealth to circumvent enemy radars, American forces repeatedly launched cruise missiles and dropped guided bombs on an ever-widening array of targets, starting with air-defence and command-and-control installations, and proceeding to critical military and industrial facilities. The brutal, paralysing efficiency of its initial strikes gave the US a decisive advantage, clearing the way for follow-on attacks that defeated opponents quickly and with minimal loss of American lives.

In addition to a careful study of this new way of war, PLA analysts sought to assess key features of the strategic environment in which US and Chinese forces might engage. In the words of one widely circulated textbook, 'the most salient objective reality that the PLA will face in future campaign operations is the fact that it will be using inferior weapons to deal with an enemy that has superior arms.'[16] Fortunately for China, however, technology alone would not be decisive. In an actual conflict, especially one fought on China's doorstep, the enemy would not have 'comprehensive superiority in politics, diplomacy, geography, and support'.[17] To the contrary, the US would have to project its forces over very long distances, which would

Table 1. **Reconnaissance–strike complex: operational requirements**

	Reconnaissance	Strike
Offence	Acquire	Disable/destroy
Defence	Deny	Protect

take time, and it would be heavily dependent on gaining access to bases and facilities on the soil of its regional allies, which could not be guaranteed. Even with local support, US forces would have to operate at the end of highly extended logistical and communications networks. Last but not least, in some of the more obvious contingencies (such as those involving Taiwan), the issues at stake would be less important to Washington than to Beijing. Regardless of its material advantages, US resolve might prove weak, especially if it were confronted with the prospect of high casualties. All of these factors have created vulnerabilities that a clever and resourceful enemy could exploit.

When combined with an assessment of US capabilities and doctrine, this analysis of technological trends, geographical constants and political variables yielded a set of four operational requirements that the PLA would have to fulfil if it were to emerge victorious from a future clash (see Table 1).

Reconnaissance battle

Based on an examination of Chinese doctrinal writings and an assessment of publicly available information about procurement and research programmes, US Air Force analyst Mark Stokes concluded in 1999 that the foundation of the PLA's emerging doctrine was 'the concept of information dominance'.[18] Stokes noted that 'Chinese military planners appear to be striving for a comparative advantage in the ability to control, collect, process, act upon, and disseminate information, giving the PLA a future edge in conflicts around its periphery.'[19] Gaining such a position of advantage would require Chinese forces to win the reconnaissance battle with an opponent at the very outset of hostilities. In short, as well as acquiring precise, up-to-date information on the location and disposition of an opponent's forces, the PLA would need to do whatever it could to deny the same kind of data to its enemies.

Strike and counter-strike

As important as it was, information dominance was 'not a goal but a means'.[20] Gaining it would permit the PLA to carry out its own strike operations, while easing the task of defending against an enemy's attacks. Data on the location of fixed installations and mobile forces would guide Chinese weapons to their targets. Meanwhile, degrading an enemy's reconnaissance systems, while at the same time destroying some portion of its strike forces, would enhance the effectiveness of China's active and passive defences (which would have fewer incoming weapons to intercept or withstand) and greatly increase the survivability of its mobile targets (which would become much more difficult for a partially blinded enemy to find).

Hitting first

The necessity of defeating an opposing RSC placed a premium on landing the first blow. This was among the most important lessons of the First Gulf War. According to analysis published in 1996, Saddam Hussein's forces 'suffered from passive strategic guidance and overlooked the importance of seizing the initiative and launching a preemptive attack'.[21] By permitting the Americans to deploy and assemble their forces securely before launching a devastating first strike, the Iraqis 'missed a good opportunity' to at least hinder the US build-up.[22] If confronted by the imminent possibility of war with the US, China could not afford to make the same mistake.

Given the overall technological superiority of US forces, and the potentially disastrous consequences of allowing them to

land the first blow, Chinese strategists believed that they had
to seize 'battlefield information dominance' through 'active
information attack with initiative'.[23] Summing up a decade's
worth of writings on the subject, Mark Stokes concluded that
the PLA's preferred method for beginning a war would be to
use missiles to launch massive, surprise 'key point strikes'.
Targets would include 'C3I nodes, weapons control centers,
high value air assets on the ground, logistics bases ... important sea combat platforms ... air bases [and] logistics bases'.[24]
In the words of one Chinese author, the primary aim of such
attacks would not be, as in more traditional forms of warfare,
the conquest of territory or the physical annihilation of enemy
forces, 'but rather the paralyzing of the other side's information system, and the destruction of the other side's will to
resist'.[25]

ASCEL

Although they do not use the term, Chinese doctrinal writings
describe operations and tactics that are entirely consistent
with the American concept of anti-access/area denial (A2/
AD). As Anton Wishik points out, 'the closest approximation
to A2/AD within the realm of Chinese open-source literature
is the PLA's "Active Strategic Counterattacks on Exterior
Lines" (ASCEL).'[26] The thinking behind ASCEL was laid out
in a 2001 article by Major-General Peng Guangjian, a senior
theorist at the Academy of Military Sciences (AMS), as well
as being incorporated into *Science of Military Strategy*, an
authoritative AMS doctrinal textbook published during the
same year. These writings represent a distillation and codi-
fication of the ideas that had emerged over the course of the
preceding decade.

The ASCEL doctrine calls for Chinese forces to strike first,
strike deep and hit hard against an approaching enemy. While

insisting that their country will never 'fire the first shot', PLA theorists go on to point out that:

> The 'first shot' at the political and strategic level is differ-
> ent from the 'first shot' at the tactical level ... As soon
> as someone violates another country's sovereignty and
> territorial integrity, they have bestowed the opposition
> the right to 'fire the first shot' at the tactical level.[27]

In other words, as soon as Beijing judges that another country has encroached on its sovereignty in any way (presumably, this includes providing political support for 'splittists'), it is entitled to initiate 'defensive military operations'.[28]

The fact that it will likely face a better-equipped force makes it imperative that the PLA 'dominate the enemy by striking first'.[29] Instead of 'passively waiting', Chinese forces must 'strive to strike the enemy at the greatest possible distance after war breaks out'. It is vital that China push its 'forward defensive positions out as far as possible, the farther the better'. Fortunately for the Chinese, long-range strike capabilities now exist, allowing them to 'strike the enemy at a great distance. If we wait at home, it is all over.'[30]

In striking deep, China would aim not only at the enemy's forces, but at the command, control and logistical infrastructure that supports them. These are potentially vulnerable points whose destruction can have decisive consequences. Thus, 'to the greatest extent possible, the war should be brought to the enemy's bases, war-fighting platforms and ... places of origin.'[31] While published writings do not define the precise location of China's 'exterior lines' within which opening strikes are to be carried out, these are generally assumed to lie at or beyond the first island chain, an imaginary line extending southward from Japan through Taiwan to the South China Sea (see Map 1).

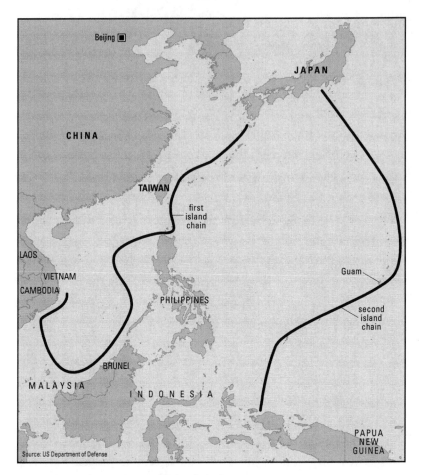

Map 1. **China's first and second island chain**

Capabilities

China has been engaged in an expansion of its military capabilities for over two decades. Defence spending jumped by 15%
in the aftermath of the Tiananmen protests and has continued
to grow at or near double-digit rates in every year since.[32] Even
allowing for the effects of inflation, the increases in real terms are
impressive, averaging over 11% per year for the 2002–11 period.
At least as remarkable as its scope and duration is the fact that, so
far, China's build-up has been essentially 'burdenless'. Because

Table 2. **Reconnaissance strike: missions and systems**

	Reconnaissance	Strike
Offence	• Command, control, communications, computers, intelligence, surveillance and reconnaissance (C4ISR) • Over-the-horizon (OTH) radars • Satellites • Unmanned aerial vehicles (UAV)	• Ballistic missiles • Cruise missiles • Torpedoes
Defence	• Anti-satellite (ASAT) systems • Camouflage, concealment and deception (CCD) • Cyber • Electronic warfare (EW) • Mobility • Operational security (OPSEC)	• Anti-submarine warfare (ASW) • Ballistic-missile defence • Hardening of structures and systems • Integrated air-defence system (IADS)

the nation's economy has also been growing rapidly, the military's share of GDP has not increased, and may actually have declined slightly in recent years. Even as it modernises its armed forces and enhances their capabilities, China continues to spend less than 2% of its total output on defence.[33]

The PLA has put the steady stream of resources it receives to a wide variety of uses, some of which are not directly related to the A2/AD mission. However, as Roger Cliff points out:

> Comparing the military capabilities China has acquired over the past decade or so with the force employment concepts found in Chinese writings ... one cannot but be impressed by the systematic and methodical way in which the PLA has gone about acquiring the capabilities needed to successfully implement those concepts.[34]

In sum, China's military has made progress towards acquiring systems that, at least on paper, have the capacity to perform each of the four missions described above: locating and striking an opponent's targets, while denying the enemy information and defending vital Chinese targets against attacks. Some of the weapons systems and other programmes associated with the performance of these tasks are listed in Table 2.

Offence–reconnaissance

By the end of the 1990s the PLA had only a very limited capacity to acquire and distribute militarily useful information about events beyond its borders. After a decade marked by launch failures and heavy dependence on assistance from foreign firms, its space-based reconnaissance capabilities had been 'slow to develop'.[35] Today, the situation has been dramatically altered. Between 2001 and 2011, the PRC reportedly launched '32 reconnaissance satellites that could be used for military targeting and tactical support'.[36] In 2012 alone, it conducted an additional 18 space launches, including six navigation satellites and 11 new remote-sensing satellites capable of performing both civil and military functions. By 2015, China will have placed a total of 100 satellites into orbit.[37]

Along with its space-based systems, the PLA has been developing and deploying UAVs at what a recent report by the US Defense Science Board describes as an 'alarming' pace.[38] China currently has at least 18 unmanned aircraft systems with varying ranges deployed or under development.[39] The People's Liberation Army Navy (PLAN) is also improving its capacity to locate distant targets with over-the-horizon (OTH) radars. According to the US Department of Defense (DoD), these large, land-based systems can be used 'in conjunction with imagery satellites to assist in locating targets at great distances from PRC shores to support long range precision strikes, including by anti-ship ballistic missiles'.[40]

As of the late 1990s, the PLA had taken only first steps toward forming a national, integrated command, control, communications, computers and intelligence (C4I) system.[41] Here too, the progress made over the past decade has been striking. In the words of the DoD's 2013 report on Chinese military capabilities, 'new technologies allow the PLA to share intelligence, battlefield information, logistics information, weather reports etc. simultaneously (over robust and redundant communications networks), resulting in improved situational awareness for commanders.' These advances are described as having 'greatly enhanced the PLA's flexibility and responsiveness'. The 'sharing of near-real-time ISR [intelligence, surveillance and reconnaissance] data with commanders in the field' eases decision-making and shortens command timelines. Such enhancements in the collection, fusion and distribution of data are deemed essential for the joint operations required to execute A2/AD.[42]

One area in which Chinese reconnaissance capabilities lag is the acquisition of targeting information essential for anti-submarine warfare (ASW). A 2009 survey by the US Office of Naval Intelligence described China's capabilities in this area as marginal.[43] While the PLAN has begun to invest in the underwater sensors, dedicated fixed-wing aircraft, helicopters and surface vessels necessary to locate and track enemy submarines, it has yet to address its shortcomings in ASW.[44]

Offence–strike

On land and on the ocean's surface, if not beneath it, Chinese commanders can see what is going on in an ever-wider area around them and, increasingly, can hit what they see. In 2000, the PLA's Second Artillery Force had only a 'nascent capacity for conventional short-range ballistic missile (SRBM) strikes against Taiwan'. By the end of the decade, it had built its conventional missile forces into one of its 'primary instruments of coercion, not only of Taiwan but of other regional neighbors'.[45] In addition to an estimated 1,100 SRBMs aimed at Taiwan, the Second Artillery Force has deployed a limited

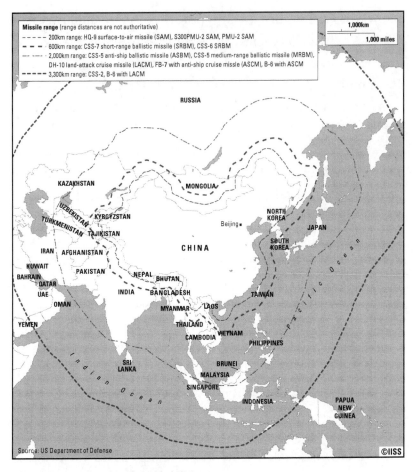

Map 2. **Conventional-strike capabilities**

but growing number of conventionally armed, medium-range ballistic missiles (MRBM).[46] Notable among these are the DF-21D anti-ship ballistic missile (ASBM) and the DF-21C MRBM, the latter intended for use against fixed targets. Both are thought to be equipped with terminally guided, conventional warheads and to have ranges of roughly 1,000 nautical miles. They are thus capable of striking targets anywhere within the first island chain, including bases and facilities in South Korea, the Philippines, Okinawa and throughout the home islands of Japan.[47] Chinese engineers are already working on a follow-on to the DF-21 that could reach as far as Guam. This island is the westernmost American territory in the Pacific and, in part because it is beyond the range of existing missiles, in recent years, has been built up into a major operational hub for US air and naval forces.[48]

In the early 1990s, deeply impressed by the performance of US *Tomahawk* cruise missiles in the First Gulf War, the PLA intensified its efforts to acquire weapons with similar capabilities.[49] Today, Chinese forces are equipped with land- and air-launched cruise missiles designed to strike targets on the ground, as well as an assortment of anti-ship cruise missiles (ASCMs) that can be fired from land, aircraft, submarines and surface vessels. In 2009, the Second Artillery Force began to deploy the DH-10 land-attack cruise missile, a long-range weapon that bears a resemblance to the American *Tomahawk* and the Russian Kh-55 cruise missiles. With a reach equivalent to the DF-21 ballistic missile, the DH-10's comparative accuracy and large conventional warhead makes it a capable land-attack weapon.[50]

For its part, the PLAN has or is acquiring as many as a dozen ASCM types.[51] Some of these are older weapons, based on Soviet, Cold War-era designs; others are modelled on the French *Exocet* and the American *Harpoon* anti-ship missiles, and can be fired at ranges of less than 100 miles from aircraft, surface ships and submarines. The PLAN has acquired ASCMs from Russia: the SS-N-22 *Sunburn* and the SS-N-27B *Sizzler*. The former is deployed on-board the navy's *Sovremmeny*-class destroyers, while the latter is part of the weaponry of the *Kilo*-class diesel submarine. The *Sunburn* is supersonic at low level, while the *Sizzler* uses a rocket-powered dart accelerated to supersonic speed for the terminal phase of an engagement, after subsonic cruise to within 20km of the target. Given their velocity, both missiles provide little time for shipboard defences to engage.[52]

Chinese submarines are also equipped with various types of torpedoes, including, according to some reports, the *Shkval*, a unique, rocket-powered model purchased from Russia that can travel at five times the speed of normal undersea weapons.[53]

Defence–reconnaissance

China's growing capacity for conventional precision-strike contributes to its ability to defend itself against hostile reconnaissance. Physically damaging or destroying some of the terrestrial, forward-based portions of the US global C4ISR network will make it more difficult for American commanders to obtain the information they need to target weapons, assess damage and communicate in a timely fashion with their forces. But this is only the start. The PLA is also working to perfect an assortment of other 'hard' and 'soft' techniques for achieving similar ends.

Chinese assessments of the First Gulf War noted that, thanks in part to its proclivity for 'expeditionary' operations conducted far from its home territory, the US military was overwhelmingly dependent on space.[54] This reliance on satellites for command, control and intelligence was a great strength, but also a potential weakness – one that PLA analysts have since described as the United States' Achilles' heel, or 'soft ribs'.[55] During the 1990s, the discussion of whether, and how, to strike at this potential point of vulnerability was largely theoretical. In recent years, however, it has become apparent that China has a variety of active anti-satellite programmes in different stages of development.[56] In 2007, the PLA tested a ground-launched 'direct-ascent' anti-satellite (ASAT) prototype. The collision of this vehicle with an ageing weather satellite produced a cloud of dangerous debris and a subsequent storm of international controversy.[57] Since then, Beijing has been more circumspect, avoiding the actual destruction of targets in space, but it is thought to have conducted at least two more test launches of rockets capable of carrying out this mission, one in 2010 and the other in 2013.[58] Recent public testimony by the commander of US Pacific Command confirms the US view that China is continuing work on a purpose-built ASAT missile system.[59] Along with so-called 'kinetic-kill' weapons, the PLA is developing, and has reportedly tested, high-powered, ground-based lasers that can be used to 'dazzle' satellite sensors. In the words of one expert, Chinese engineers are also 'relentlessly focused' on developing 'diverse forms of electronic attack' to disrupt the links between orbiting satellites and their ground stations.[60]

Jamming communication with satellites is only one part of a much larger effort to employ EW in order to reduce or eliminate US technological advantages.[61] In addition to attacking C4ISR nodes with what are referred to as 'hard weapons', Chinese writings have long stressed 'the use of electronic means of jamming or the use of antiradiation (missile) ... weapons to attack enemy information and intelligence collection systems such as communications and radar'.[62] PLA doctrine describes the electromagnetic spectrum as the fourth dimension of warfare, equivalent in importance to ground, sea and air, and the military is developing, testing and deploying EW weapons designed to 'suppress or deceive enemy electronic equipment', including radar, communications and navigation systems.[63]

The PLA's interest in 'computer virus warfare' extends back to at least the early 1990s, when its analysts concluded that the US had inserted malign code into the software of Iraq's air-defence computers.[64] Since 2001, China's cyber activities have increased greatly in volume and sophistication.[65] A PLA unit tasked with penetrating foreign computer networks is believed to have begun operation in 2006.[66] In the last few years, intrusions linked to China have grown to the point where they have become a major concern to both government and industry in the US, as well as in other countries.[67] In its 2013 report on Chinese military activities, the DoD took the unprecedented step of stating publicly that at least some of the recent flood of intrusions was 'attributable directly to the Chinese government and military'.[68] In June 2013, the problem had grown to such dimensions that President Barack Obama raised it in his first summit meeting with newly appointed Chinese leader Xi Jinping.[69]

If Chinese hackers can steal data from highly protected government and military computer systems in peacetime, they may also be able to shut them down in the event of war. As the DoD points out, 'the skills required for these intrusions are similar to those necessary to conduct computer network attacks.'[70] Among other potentially devastating effects, operations of this kind could cripple the ability of American military and intelligence organisations to communicate with one another, and to gather and distribute information vital to the conduct of operations against China. Successful cyber attacks could thus render US forces deaf, dumb and blind in the opening moments of a war. Acknowledging the severity of the threat, a report by the Defense Science Board in early 2013 concluded bluntly that, 'the United States cannot be confident that our critical Information Technology (IT) [systems] will work under attack from a sophisticated and well-resourced opponent.'[71]

Because they also rely heavily on computer networks and other modern communications systems, China's military and government organisations are themselves increasingly vulnerable to penetration and exploitation. Recognising this fact, planners have taken steps to try to protect critical information from prying foreign eyes and ears. The national fibre-optic communications network put in place since the 1990s is, by design, far less vulnerable to signals-intelligence collection than it would be if it made extensive use of microwave or other radio

-frequency transmissions. An emphasis on operational security and the rigorous restriction and protection of information have deep roots in Chinese strategic culture, and remain prominent features of training and operations at all levels.[72] PLA theorists and planners continue to stress concealment, camouflage and deception (CCD) – closely related concepts that are also 'ingrained into traditional Chinese strategic constructs'.[73]

Movement provides a final means of shielding vital capabilities from hostile surveillance. Experience has shown that even a sophisticated opponent such as the US can have difficulty in locating and tracking continually mobile targets. Unsurprisingly, therefore, as China's concerns about the United States' RSC have grown, Beijing has deployed more of its own strike assets on mobile launchers. This is true of short- and medium-range conventional ballistic missiles, conventionally armed land-attack cruise missiles and an increasing portion of China's small, but growing, force of nuclear-tipped ICBMs. The submarine-launched ballistic missiles that the PLAN recently began to deploy enjoy the combined benefits of mobility and underwater concealment.[74]

Defence–strike

Even if it can disrupt the enemy's reconnaissance capabilities, while finding and hitting its bases and forces across the Western Pacific, China will undoubtedly have to absorb at least some strikes against targets in its own territory. Defending against such attacks remains a vital mission, and will be even more important and challenging if the US somehow manages to land the first blow. PLA planners have long regarded the United States' conventional precision-strike capabilities with a mix of respect and fear; over the last two decades, they have gone to considerable lengths to try to blunt their effectiveness.

As with other aspects of its build-up, Beijing has been

pursuing multiple, complementary approaches to achieve core objectives. With an air-defence system that was widely regarded as antiquated, following the First Gulf War, Chinese policymakers began to place 'high priority on upgrading their overall defense capability to protect strategically critical points'.[75] In the mid-1990s, the People's Liberation Army Air Force (PLAAF) began to deploy a variety of modern, long-range surface-to-air missiles, some purchased from Russia and others indigenously developed. After a procurement deal with Israel collapsed under US pressure in 2000, Chinese designers subsequently built, and have begun to field, their own airborne warning-and-control aircraft.[76] These systems are key components in what is becoming an integrated air-defence system (IADS): a 'multilayered defense consisting of weapons systems, radars and C4ISR platforms working together to counter multiple types of air threats of various ranges and altitudes', including 'precision strike munitions ... launched from long distances'.[77] Despite having made progress in defending against some types of air-breathing platforms, the PLAAF continues to work on the problem of detecting and tracking stealthy manned and unmanned aircraft, and it does not yet have a workable ballistic-missile-defence system.[78]

Aware that some weapons will always get through, Chinese planners have made substantial investments in passive-defence measures. This is not an entirely new trend. During the 1960s and 1970s, Beijing expended vast resources to protect critical targets from nuclear attack, including through the use of caves to hide missiles, the construction of deep underground bunkers and command posts, and, most remarkably, a hugely wasteful and inefficient programme for the nationwide dispersal of its defence-industrial base.[79] As the Cold War wound down, China began to consider modernising its network of underground facilities (UGF). This process 'took on a renewed urgency following China's observation of US and NATO air operations' in Serbia and during the First Gulf War. According to the Pentagon, these campaigns convinced Beijing that 'it needed to build more survivable, deeply-buried facilities', and resulted in a 'widespread UGF construction effort detected throughout China' during the first decade of the twenty-first century.[80]

Conclusion

While these defensive measures suggest that China is preparing to absorb an enemy attack, and perhaps even a first strike, it is clearly building an RSC that will work best if it is used first. This conclusion is not surprising; it is a reflection both of the imperatives of PLA doctrine and the inherent difficulties involved in performing certain military tasks. There is little reason to doubt China's capacity to deliver precise conventional strikes against fixed, pre-targeted points across East Asia. Provided that their reconnaissance networks remain intact, China's air, naval and missile forces will also be able to pose an increasingly credible threat to US and allied surface vessels within the first island chain, and eventually beyond it.

Defending against American strikes, on the other hand, will likely remain a challenge for some time to come. While China's IADS is impressive in comparison to what came before, and while it clearly has serious capabilities against some types of aircraft, its ability to detect and intercept ballistic missiles or stealthy aircraft and cruise missiles appears, at this point, to be limited. As for undersea defence, the PLAN's deficits in ASW mean that it would be hard pressed to prevent hostile submarines and unmanned underwater vehicles from operating close to its shores.

China's reconnaissance network has also improved markedly in the past decade, but portions of it remain vulnerable to attack by a sophisticated foe. By their nature, OTH radar antennas are big, exposed and fragile structures; yet they appear, at this point, to be crucial to China's ability to track and target American aircraft carriers. Satellite downlink stations and launch facilities are also comparatively 'soft' and few in number. While the US government has highlighted Chinese investments in anti-satellite and cyber-warfare capabilities, the Pentagon has also been active on these fronts.[81] If it lets the other side land the first blow, the PLA could find itself, if not totally blind, then with its situational awareness severely diminished.

On the defensive side, the PLA's ASAT capabilities are nascent but growing, thanks to continuing investment and multiple programmes. By all accounts, China is an early adopter of computer-network attacks. Recent official statements and authoritative reports suggest that the US government is deeply concerned about the possibility of a 'cyber Pearl Harbor'.[82] Lingering uncertainties about the size of its nuclear forces and the unexpected appearance, in recent years, of several new weapons systems (such as the J-20 stealth fighter and the *Yuan*-class attack submarine) suggest that, even in an era of ubiquitous reconnaissance, China retains some of its traditional strengths in concealment and deception.[83] Needless to say, such techniques would be all the more effective against an enemy whose capabilities had first been diminished by offensive means.

Notes

[1] David Shambaugh, *Modernizing China's Military: Progress, Problems, and Prospects* (Berkeley, CA: University of California Press, 2002), pp. 64–5.

[2] Andrew J. Nathan and Robert S. Ross, *The Great Wall and the Empty Fortress: China's Search for Security* (New York: W.W. Norton & Company, 1997), p. 72.

[3] This term was introduced in 1993. See Roger Cliff et al., *Entering the Dragon's Lair: Chinese Antiaccess Strategies and Their Implications for the United States* (Santa Monica, CA: RAND Corporation, 2007), p.

21, http://www.rand.org/content/dam/rand/pubs/monographs/2007/RAND_MG524.pdf.

4   See, for example, the 1994 article, Shen Kuigan, 'Dialectics of Defeating the Superior with the Inferior', excerpted in Michael Pillsbury (ed.), *Chinese Views of Future Warfare* (Honolulu, HI: University Press of the Pacific, 2002), pp. 213–9.

5   See Robert S. Ross, 'The 1995-96 Taiwan Strait Confrontation: Coercion, Credibility, and the Use of Force', *International Security*, vol. 25, no. 2, Autumn 2000, pp. 87–123.

6   Aaron L. Friedberg, *A Contest for Supremacy: China, America and the Struggle for Mastery in Asia* (New York: W. W. Norton & Company, 2011), pp. 97–8.

7   Shambaugh, *Modernizing China's Military*, pp. 3–4.

8   See the discussion of the 1995–96 crisis in Andrew Scobell, *China's Use of Military Force: Beyond the Great Wall and the Long March* (New York: Cambridge University Press, 2003), pp. 171–91.

9   Bernard D. Cole, *The Great Wall at Sea: China's Navy in the Twenty-First Century* (Annapolis, MD: Naval Institute Press, 2010), p. 98.

10 Mark Stokes, 'China's Evolving Conventional Strategic Strike Capability: The anti-ship ballistic missile challenge to US maritime operations in the Western Pacific and beyond', Project 2049 Institute, 14 September 2009, p. 20, http://project2049.net/documents/chinese_anti_ship_ballistic_missile_asbm.pdf.

11 Keith L. Shimko, *The Iraq Wars and America's Military Revolution* (New York: Cambridge University Press, 2010), p. 121.

12 Chinese assessments of the Kosovo War are discussed in June Teufel Dreyer, 'People's Liberation Army Lessons From Foreign Conflicts: The Air War in Kosovo', in Andrew Scobell, David Lai and Roy Kamphausen (eds), *Chinese Lessons From Other Peoples' Wars* (Carlisle, PA: Strategic Studies Institute, November 2011), pp. 33–74.

13 David M. Finkelstein, 'China Reconsiders Its National Security: "The Great Peace and Development Debate of 1999"', Project Asia, CNA Corporation, December 2000, p. 3, https://cna.org/sites/default/files/research/D0014464.A1.pdf.

14 Dreyer, 'People's Liberation Army Lessons From Foreign Conflicts', p. 41. See also Shambaugh, *Modernizing China's Military*, pp. 87–8.

15 David Shambaugh reports that, in addition to 'scores of symposia', and numerous articles in professional journals and the official PLA newspaper *Jiefangjun*, by the late 1990s, military publishing houses had released nearly 300 volumes on topics related to high-tech warfare. Shambaugh, *Modernizing China's Military*, p. 71.

16 Wang Houqing and Zhang Xingye (eds), *Science of Campaigns* (Beijing: National Defense University Press, 2000), cited in James C. Mulvenon et al., *Chinese Responses to US Military Transformation and Implications for the Department of Defense* (Santa Monica, CA: RAND Corporation, 2006), p. 47.

17 See the 1997 monograph, 'Modern Strategy for Using the Inferior to

Defeat the Superior', cited in Cliff et al., *Entering the Dragon's Lair*, p. 27.

18 Mark A. Stokes, *China's Strategic Modernization: Implications for the United States* (Carlisle, PA: Strategic Studies Institute, 1999), p. 9.

19 *Ibid.*, p. 58.

20 Zhang Yuliang (ed.), *Science of Campaigns* (Beijing: National Defense University Press, 2006), p. 176.

21 Quote from a 1996 article entitled 'Preemptive Strikes Crucial in Limited High-Tech Wars', cited in Cliff et al., *Entering the Dragon's Lair*, p. 32.

22 *Ibid.*

23 Yuliang (ed.), *The Science of Campaigns*, p. 183.

24 Stokes, *China's Strategic Modernization*, p. 97.

25 See the 1996 article, 'The Third Military Revolution', translated in Pillsbury (ed.), *Chinese Views of Future Warfare*, p. 393.

26 Anton Lee Wishik II, 'An Anti-Access Approximation: The PLA's Active Strategic Counterattacks on Exterior Lines', *China Security*, no. 19, 2011, p. 38.

27 *Ibid.*, p. 41.

28 *Ibid.*

29 Peng Guangqian and Yao Youzhi (eds), *Science of Military Strategy* (Beijing: Military Science Publishing House, 2005), p. 384.

30 Wishik, 'An Anti-Access Approximation', p. 42.

31 *Ibid.*

32 Shambaugh, *Modernizing China's Military*, p. 189.

33 For an overview of various measures, see Adam P. Liff and Andrew S. Erickson, 'Demystifying China's Defence Spending: Less Mysterious in the Aggregate', *China Quarterly*, vol. 216, March 2013, pp. 1–26.

34 Roger Cliff, 'Anti-Access Measures in Chinese Defense Strategy', testimony for the US–China Economic and Security Review Commission, 27 January 2011, http://www.rand.org/pubs/testimonies/CT354.html.

35 Stokes, *China's Strategic Modernization*, p. 35.

36 Eric Hagt and Matthew Durnin, 'Space, China's Tactical Frontier', *Journal of Strategic Studies*, vol. 34, no. 5, October 2011, p. 736.

37 Office of the Secretary of Defense, *Annual Report to Congress: Military and Security Developments Involving the People's Republic of China 2013* (Washington DC: Office of the Secretary of Defense, 2013), pp. 9, 65.

38 Defense Science Board, *Task Force Report: The Role of Autonomy in DoD Systems* (Washington DC: DoD, 2012), p. 71.

39 Most of the unmanned aircraft currently deployed are shorter-range, tactical systems, but longer-range platforms are under development. For a list of these, see David Shlapak, 'Equipping the PLAAF: The Long March to Modernity', in Richard P. Hallion, Roger Cliff and Phillip C. Saunder (eds), *The Chinese Air Force: Evolving Concepts, Roles, and Capabilities* (Washington DC: National Defense University, 2012), p. 199.

40 Office of the Secretary of Defense, *Annual Report to Congress: Military and Security Developments Involving the People's Republic of China 2010* (Washington DC: Office of the Secretary of Defense, 2010), p. 2.

41 Stokes, *China's Strategic Modernization*, p. 43.

42 Office of the Secretary of Defense, *Military and Security Developments Involving the People's Republic of China 2013*, p. 34.

43 Office of Naval Intelligence, *The People's Liberation Army Navy: A Modern Navy with Chinese Characteristics* (Suitland, MD: Office of Naval Intelligence, 2009), p. 17.

44 See Lyle Goldstein, 'Beijing Confronts Long-Standing Weaknesses in Anti-Submarine Warfare', *China Brief*, vol. 11, no. 14, 29 July 2011.

45 Office of the Secretary of Defense, *Annual Report to Congress: Military Power of the People's Republic of China, 2009* (Washington DC: Office of the Secretary of Defense, 2009), p. IX.

46 Office of the Secretary of Defense, *Military and Security Developments Involving the People's Republic of China 2013*, p. 5.

47 The US Air Force estimates that China has 'fewer than 30' DF-21Cs and an unknown number of DF-21Ds. National Air and Space Intelligence Center, 'Ballistic and Cruise Missile Threat', 2013, p. 17, http://www.afisr.af.mil/shared/media/document/AFD-130710-054.pdf.

48 Mark A. Stokes and Ian Easton, 'Evolving Aerospace Trends in the Asia-Pacific Region: Implications for Stability in the Taiwan Strait and Beyond', Project 2049 Institute, 27 May 2010, p.16, http://project2049.net/documents/aerospace_trends_asia_pacific_region_stokes_easton.pdf.

49 Stokes, *China's Strategic Modernization*, p. 80.

50 Carlo Kopp and Martin Andrew, 'PLA Cruise Missiles; PLA Air-Surface Missiles', Air Power Australia, April 2012, http://www.ausairpower.net/APA-PLA-Cruise-Missiles.html. See also Ian Easton, 'The Assassin Under the Radar: China's DH-10 Cruise Missile Program', Project 2049 Institute, 1 October 2009, http://project2049.net/documents/assassin_under_radar_china_cruise_missile.pdf.

51 Office of the Secretary of Defense, *Military and Security Developments Involving the People's Republic of China 2013*, p. 42.

52 In 2007, former DoD officials complained publicly that, 'after nearly 6 years of warnings', the US Navy had yet to come up with a satisfactory plan for defending its ships against the *Sizzler*. Tony Capaccio, 'Navy Lacks Plan to Defend Against "Sizzler" Missile', Bloomberg, 23 March 2007, http://web.archive.org/web/20071119102801/http://www.bloomberg.com/apps/news?pid=20601070&sid=a5LkaUowj714&refer=home.

53 Peter Truscott, *Kursk: Russia's Lost Pride* (London: Simon and Schuster, 2002), pp. 119–21. Despite its terrifying speed, the effectiveness of the *Skhval* is limited by the fact that it is unguided and so must be fired at relatively close range.

54 According to a 1994 study by the Academy of Military Science, the Americans were dependent on space for 70% of their communications overall, 90% of naval communications and 90% of intelligence collection. Stokes, *China's Military Modernization*, p. 117.

55 The latter phrase is from an article published by a Chinese author in 2000, quoted in Ashley J. Tellis, 'China's Military Space Strategy', *Survival*, vol. 49, no. 3, Autumn 2007, p. 49.

56 See Michael Pillsbury, 'An Assessment of China's Anti-Satellite and Space Warfare Programs, Policies and Doctrines', report prepared for the US–China Economic and Security Review Commission, 19 January 2007, http://origin.www.uscc.gov/sites/default/files/Research/An%20Assessment%20of%20China%27s%20Anti-Satellite%20And%20Space%20Warfare%20Programs.pdf.

57 See Shirley Kan, *China's Anti-Satellite Weapon Test* (Washington DC: Congressional Research Service, April 2007).

58 Brian Weeden, 'Time for Obama To Go Public on China's ASAT Program', *Defense News*, 2 June 2013, http://www.defensenews.com/article/20130602/DEFREG/306020009/Time-Obama-Go-Public-China-s-ASAT-Program.

59 Statement by Samuel Locklear before the Senate Armed Services Committee, 'The Posture of the US Pacific Command and US Strategic Command', 9 April 2013, http://www.pacom.mil/commander/statements-testimony/20130409-hasc-uspacom-posture-opening-statement.shtml.

60 Tellis, 'China's Military Space Strategy', pp. 56–8.

61 Office of the Secretary of Defense, *Military and Security Developments Involving the People's Republic of China 2013*, p. 37.

62 See the 1995 article, 'Information Warfare', translated in Pillsbury, *Chinese Views of Future Warfare*, p. 329.

63 Office of the Secretary of Defense, *Military and Security Developments Involving the People's Republic of China 2013*, p. 37.

64 On Chinese assessments of the use of cyber attacks during the First Gulf War, see Kevin Pollpeter, 'Controlling the Information Domain: Space, Cyber, and Electronic Warfare', in Ashley J. Tellis and Travis Tanner (eds), *Strategic Asia 2012–2013: China's Military Challenge* (Seattle, WA: National Bureau of Asian Research, 2012), p. 174.

65 *Ibid.*

66 The activities of Unit 61398 are described in the report of an American computer security firm. Mandiant Intelligence Center, 'APT1: Exposing One of China's Cyber Espionage Units' (Alexandria, VA; Mandiant, February 2013), http://intelreport.mandiant.com/Mandiant_APT1_Report.pdf.

67 See the discussion in National Bureau of Asian Research, *The Report of the Commission on the Theft of American Intellectual Property* (Seattle, WA: National Bureau of Asian Research, 2013).

68 Office of the Secretary of Defense, *Military and Security Developments Involving the People's Republic of China 2013*, p. 36.

69 Aamer Madhani, 'Obama presses Xi on cybersecurity at Sunnylands summit', *USA Today*, 9 June 2013, http://www.usatoday.com/story/news/politics/2013/06/07/obama-xi-sunnylands-summit/2402397/.

[70] Office of the Secretary of Defense, *Military and Security Developments Involving the People's Republic of China 2013*, p. 36.

[71] While the unclassified version of the DSB report did not name names, the identity of at least one such opponent was obvious. Defense Science Board, *Task Force Report: Resilient Military Systems and the Advanced Cyber Threat* (Washington DC: Defense Science Board, January 2013), p. 1.

[72] Mulvenon et al., *Chinese Responses to US Military Transformation and Implications for the Department of Defense*, pp. xv, 138.

[73] Stokes, *China's Military Modernization*, p. 57.

[74] China has reportedly deployed upwards of 25 DF-31 road-mobile ICBMs. National Air and Space Intelligence Center, 'Ballistic and Cruise Missile Threat', p. 21. Beijing's JL-2 SLBM reached initial operational capability in 2013. Office of the Secretary of Defense, *Military and Security Developments Involving the People's Republic of China 2013*, p. 31. Some analysts have recently suggested that China may be concealing a sizeable cache of nuclear warheads and missiles in a vast complex of underground tunnels. See Philip A. Karber, 'Strategic Implications of China's Underground Great Wall', Asian Arms Control Project, Georgetown University, 26 September 2011, http://www.fas.org/nuke/guide/china/Karber_UndergroundFacilities-Full_2011_reduced.pdf. These claims have been disputed, primarily on the grounds that China does not

have sufficient fissile-material production capacity to manufacture large numbers of additional weapons. Jeffrey Lewis, 'Collected Thoughts on Phil Karber', Arms Control Wonk, 7 December 2011, http://lewis.armscontrolwonk.com/archive/4799/collected-thoughts-on-phil-karber.

[75] Stokes, *China's Military Modernization*, p. 109.

[76] Shlapak, 'Equipping the PLAAF', pp. 197–8, 201–2.

[77] Office of the Secretary of Defense, *Military and Security Developments Involving the People's Republic of China 2013*, p. 67.

[78] According to the DoD, 'China's existing long-range SAM inventory offers limited capability against ballistic missiles.' *Ibid.*, p. 35.

[79] On the latter, see Barry Naughton, 'The Third Front: Defense Industrialization in the Chinese Interior', *China Quarterly*, no. 115, September 1988, pp. 352–86.

[80] Office of the Secretary of Defense, *Military and Security Developments Involving the People's Republic of China 2013*, p. 31.

[81] While the Pentagon does not appear to have ASAT programmes comparable to China's, it does have some capacity to shoot down orbiting satellites. In February 2008, the US destroyed a malfunctioning satellite using an anti-ballistic missile fired from an *Aegis* cruiser. 'US shoots down toxic satellite', *Daily Telegraph*, 21 February 2008, http://web.archive.org/web/20081222024953/http://www.news.com.au/dailytelegraph/story/0,2 2049,23251796-5001028,00.html. According to press accounts,

the US is also developing options for offensive cyber operations, as well as the defence of its own computer networks. Tom Gjelten, 'First Strike: US Cyber Warriors Seize the Offensive', *World Affairs*, January/February 2013, http://www.worldaffairsjournal.org/article/first-strike-us-cyber-warriors-seize-offensive. Recent leaks by former NSA employee Edward Snowden suggest that in 2011 alone the US carried out over two hundred such operations. Barton Gellman and Ellen Nakashima, 'U.S. spy agencies mounted 231 offensive cyber-operations in 2011, documents show', *Washington Post*, 30 August 2013, http://articles.washingtonpost.com/2013-08-30/world/41620705_1_computer-worm-former-u-s- officials-obama-administration.

[82] This term was used by former Secretary of Defense Leon Panetta, among others. See 'Remarks by Secretary Panetta on Cybersecurity to the Business Executive for National Security', New York, 11 October 2012, http://www.defense.gov/transcripts/transcript.aspx?transcriptid=5136.

[83] While the J-20 was known to be in development, the timing of its initial test took Western intelligence services by surprise. Elisabeth Bumiller and Michael Wines, 'Test of Stealth Fighter Clouds Gates Visit to China', *New York Times*, 11 January 2011. According to some accounts, the US was unaware of the existence of a new class of diesel-powered submarine until a photograph of one was posted on the Internet. 'Chinese Produce New Type of Sub', *Washington Times*, 16 July 2004.

CHAPTER TWO

A belated response

The forces and doctrine described in the previous chapter present American strategists with four distinct but interrelated challenges. Firstly, the People's Liberation Army's (PLA) expanding anti-access/area-denial (A2/AD) capabilities will make it far more difficult and dangerous for the United States to intervene in a conflict on behalf of its regional friends and allies, and could conceivably deter it from doing so. As recently as the late 1990s, an American president contemplating intervention in a Taiwan contingency (or a maritime dispute between China and Japan) could rest assured that, at least in terms of the military consequences, the risks were limited to the potential loss of a few ships and aircraft, and the extremely unlikely prospect of suicidal nuclear escalation by Beijing. Today, such a decision would carry with it the danger that US aircraft carriers might be sunk, and regional bases badly damaged or destroyed, in the opening phase of a conflict. There is also at least the chance that Beijing, notwithstanding its no-first-use policy, might make limited use of nuclear weapons, perhaps believing that it had a second-strike force large and secure enough to deter all-out American retaliation. However remote these possibilities may seem in peacetime, in the event of a serious crisis, they could not help but weigh heavily on the minds of US decision-makers. Even if Washington chose eventually to intervene, equivocation and delay could enable Chinese forces to achieve a fait accompli, thereby increasing the costs and risks of subsequent US action.

Secondly, regardless of whether, in the event, Washington was dissuaded from coming to the aid of its friends, doubts about its resolve and reliability could help to undermine the efficacy of its security guarantees, thereby weakening the alliances that rest on them. A credible military strategy and the capabilities needed to back it up are essential to reassuring friends, as well as deterring enemies. China's ongoing build-up has begun to raise questions in Asia about the survivability of US forward-based forces and the viability of plans for their use. If US allies conclude that Washington no longer has the ability or the will to help them defend themselves against coercion or attack, they may feel that they have little choice but to appease China. As it seeks to deter American intervention, Beijing is thus working simultaneously to decouple the US from its regional security partners.

Thirdly, the programmes that China has been pursuing for the better part of two decades are now poised to impose disproportionate costs on the US and its allies. Compared to the targets at which they are aimed, the PLA's long-range, conventional precision-strike weapons are relatively inexpensive. American analysts have been assessing 'cost-imposing', 'competitive' strategies since the latter stages of the Cold War. In recent years, however, it is China that has been more adept at putting theory into practice.[1] In time, Beijing may hope to convince Washington that the costs of competition are too high to continue. Unable to maintain its position in the region at a reasonable price, Washington may conclude that it has no choice but to accept a new Asian regional order. The US fiscal crisis, combined with the fact that, despite a recent slowdown, China's economy continues to grow at a rapid pace, makes this goal seem more attainable than it did only a few years ago.

The fourth and final challenge posed by Beijing's build-up is the most urgent and consequential. The capabilities that China has been acquiring are not merely for show; they are intended to give the nation's leaders viable options for using force in a variety of contingencies and against a range of enemies, including the US. PLA planners are dissatisfied, no doubt, with their current preparations; they are acutely aware of their own vulnerabilities and know that there is much more work yet to be done. Still, as they look back over the last two decades, Chinese strategists have reason to feel pleased with what has been accomplished. Even if they do not think they could achieve their objectives in a conflict that broke out tomorrow, if current trends continue, their confidence is likely to grow.

Objections

Before turning to the question of whether, and why, the US has been slow to respond to these four challenges, it is necessary to consider the possibility that their imminence and severity have been exaggerated.

Capabilities

There are obvious questions regarding the likely performance of each individual piece of China's evolving A2/AD complex, and even greater uncertainties about how well the various components would work together under wartime conditions. Even the most forward-leaning analysts would probably agree with the statement, in a recent article, by Robert Ross that the Second Artillery Force has 'not yet mastered the technology' required to employ the DF-21D anti-ship ballistic missile. But it does not follow from this observation, or other similar judgements about the performance of new stealthy jet aircraft or command, control, communications, computers, intelligence, surveillance and reconnaissance (C4ISR) systems that, as Ross puts it, 'the United States has greatly overestimated China's military capabilities.'[2] In fact, the publicly available evidence suggests that the PLA has been making steady improvements in the discrimination and reliability of the sensors and communications systems that it needs to locate, track and target US and allied ships and aircraft operating far from its shores. The PLA has also improved the range, accuracy and lethality of the weapons it could use to strike at mobile, as well as fixed, targets.[3]

Debates over current capabilities sometimes obscure more important questions about prevailing trends; what matters is not only where the PLA is at present, but where it is likely to be in five or ten years' time. It may be true, for example, that China presently lacks the constellation of satellites it would need to provide near-continuous electronic, optical and radar coverage of the Western Pacific. Thus, even if the DF-21D works as advertised, and even if the PLA is able to use other means to help locate ships at sea (including over-the-horizon radars, unmanned aerial vehicles and even a flotilla of fishing trawlers equipped with GPS receivers and ship-to-shore radios or satellite phones), it probably does not yet have the kind of detailed, near-real-time targeting information it needs to make the missile into an effective weapon. That said, the number and characteristics of the satellites China has already said it intends to launch, and the possibility that it could use existing satellites in unconventional ways, suggest that it may be closer to having a viable, open-ocean surveillance capacity than some analysts assume.[4]

While there are doubtlessly many obstacles to be overcome before China's A2/AD complex can achieve its full potential, there is no reason to think that any of them are insurmountable. What is required are not fundamental breakthroughs or massive increases in funding but continued, steady, incremental improvements in the performance of individual systems and in the process of knitting them together into an effective reconnaissance–strike complex.

It is important to also remember that, at least until war breaks out, perceptions matter as much as, or more than, reality. Even if the DF-21D turns out to be a dud, the belief that it could be a game changer will influence the assessments and plans of the US, its allies and other Asian nations; indeed, it has already begun to do so.[5] What matters most, of course, is how China's military and political leaders assess their evolving capabilities. All things being equal, if they come to believe that they have a good chance of pulling off what Herman Kahn once described as a 'splendid first strike', they are more likely to try. Conversely, if they harbour deep doubts that the weapons in which they have invested so much will actually perform as planned, the leadership will be more reluctant to put them to the test and may decide to back away from a confrontation, even at the risk of incurring serious diplomatic and domestic political costs.

Intentions

Most sceptics focus less on capabilities than on intentions, arguing that even if China's leaders believed they could launch devastating conventional attacks on American and allied forces and bases across Asia, the dangers of doing so would be so great as to make them extremely unlikely ever to try. Unfortunately, there are a number of situations in which the risks of inaction might appear to exceed the risks of action. The most obvious of these is the most familiar: Beijing could some day find itself in a situation in which it decides it must take action to prevent Taiwan's independence and fears that the US is about to foil its plans by intervening. Presumably, it is because they can envision such scenarios that China's leaders have invested enormous resources over a span of almost two decades to develop military options for dealing with them.

Another common objection applies not just to the possible widespread use of A2/AD capabilities, but to virtually any form of direct conflict between China and the US or one of its advanced industrial allies. Critics note that even a tense confrontation that did not result in the actual use of force could have profoundly disruptive effects on the world economy. Referring to the magnitude of the costs that would result from economic warfare alone, one sceptic asks: 'what kind of atrocity would China have to commit before we could justify wreaking havoc on global markets?'[6] Factoring in the damage done by kinetic weapons should raise the bar even higher.

The claim that economic interdependence makes war unthinkable is familiar, as are the counters to it. To take only the most spectacular illustration: the downward spiral of relations between Germany and Great Britain after the turn of the twentieth century demonstrates that a high level of bilateral trade and investment is not always a reliable guarantor of peace.[7] More recently, Beijing has chosen to escalate long-standing maritime disputes with Tokyo, stoking public passions and permitting violent anti-Japanese protests on the streets of major cities, despite the risk of damaging relations with a vital trading partner. Even in the era of globalisation, it is clear that politics can sometimes still trump economics.

The crucial question concerns what decision-makers believe is likely rather than what turns out to be true. China's rulers may well worry about the economic consequences of a conflict with the US, especially one that becomes protracted; indeed, such fears undoubtedly add to the attraction of strategies that promise a quick victory. Playing on Beijing's anxieties about the effects of a prolonged struggle could, in fact, contribute to deterrence. As was true on the eve of the First World War, however, it would be dangerous to assume that the costs of war make it impossible.

History also suggests that leaders often underestimate the duration and cost of the conflicts they initiate. The fact that China's current concept of war with an advanced opponent relies so heavily on missiles and cyber attacks that can be launched with the push of a button, and which, if they work, could destroy their targets within minutes, may contribute to precisely this kind of miscalculation.

In addition to the possible economic effects, Chinese strategists may fear that using force in what they hope will be a limited, sharp and decisive fashion could have other unintended and undesirable consequences. Among these, the most obvious are escalation to the use of nuclear weapons and internal unrest that could threaten the survival of the Chinese Communist Party's (CCP) regime. Chinese analysts know that the US has long reserved the option of nuclear escalation should conventional means prove inadequate to defend its interests and allies. After all, the 'umbrella' that the US extends over its closest friends is nothing less than a promise to use nuclear weapons on their behalf in extremis.

PLA planners cannot be certain that the US would refrain from a nuclear response, especially to a devastatingly effective conventional first strike. Their judgement on this question will depend on their assessment of the American stake in a given confrontation, how they think US decision-makers will weigh the prospect of a possible Chinese response in kind, and any beliefs the US may have about the existence of 'firebreaks' (notional barriers that could raise the potential for escalation if crossed). Rational strategists could conceivably conclude that the US would not be willing to risk Los Angeles for Taipei by launching nuclear attacks on Chinese soil, especially if the conflict was limited to ambiguous cyber attacks, the loss of satellites to blinding or jamming, and perhaps even the sinking of a major surface combatant. It would be harder, though by no means impossible, for PLA planners to be sure that the US would not seriously consider using nuclear weapons in response to a wide-ranging conventional first strike on its forward-deployed ships, planes and regional bases.

The PLA's current concerns about nuclear escalation could, however, be lessened by the development of a bigger and more secure second-strike capability. As described in Chapter One, China is in the process of what appears, at this point, to be a relatively modest expansion in the size of its arsenal of intercontinental land- and sea-based missiles. Many foreign observers believe that this build-up is a response to US initiatives. In this view, PLA planners are trying to forestall the possibility that a combination of growing long-range conventional precision-strike capabilities and expanding missile-defence networks could some day enable the US to strip China of its capacity for nuclear retaliation.

According to some Western analysts, China's aim is 'assured retaliation', a goal that can be met by building a force sufficiently large and secure to absorb a first strike and still deliver a retaliatory blow of perhaps a few dozen nuclear weapons against an enemy's cities.[8]

Even if it is accurate, this assessment of the scope and purpose of China's nuclear modernisation programme is not reassuring. It suggests that, while they recognise the importance of nuclear deterrence, Chinese strategists may also believe that, with planned enhancements to their second-strike capability, deterrence should be relatively easy to maintain. The problem with such an attitude is that it could, in turn, encourage decision-makers to think that they can keep a conflict limited to the conventional level, even if they start it by launching a large, but still conventional, attack. If PLA planners assessed that they were well situated to deter nuclear escalation, they might, therefore, conclude that their growing A2/AD capabilities were, in fact, eminently useable. [9]

Despite its obvious economic achievements and the unmistakable growth in its military power, China continues to face a daunting array of domestic challenges. The country's leaders devote a substantial portion of their time and energy to dealing with these problems and, judging from the scale of their expenditures on police, surveillance and special security forces, are deeply fearful of internal unrest. Could anxiety about domestic instability act as an additional constraint on Beijing's propensity to use force against foreign foes?

The answer to this question depends, in part, on how China's leaders weigh the stakes in a potential conflict, and how they assess their chances of success. In some cases, concern over the domestic costs of inaction could actually make the regime more likely to use force. The prospect of a popular backlash if Taiwan seemed to be on the verge of independence is the most obvious example, but fear of the consequences of humiliation in a confrontation with Japan could also push an insecure leadership to the brink of war rather than hold it back. The fact that the CCP sees foreign conspiracies behind virtually every instance of internal unrest could also make it more prone to lash out against those it suspects of attempting to undermine its authority. China may well be an increasingly 'fragile superpower', beset by mounting domestic difficulties, but that does not necessarily mean that it will be more averse to strategic risk.[10]

On the other hand, if they are uncertain that they will achieve quick victory, fear of social instability could make

China's leaders more cautious than they would be if they had greater confidence in enduring popular support. Authoritarian rulers who launch unsuccessful military adventures face the prospect of regime collapse and an untimely demise, rather than mere removal from office at the next election.[11] Because their legitimacy so clearly rests on the provision of continuing improvements in economic welfare, China's current leaders also have special reason to fear the economic hardships and dislocations that would inevitably accompany an extended conflict. Once again, however, an important caveat is in order. The PLA's new capabilities could be appealing precisely because they seem to offer a high-tech, 'non-contact' way of avoiding the messy problem of a protracted war.

Another objection to the nightmarish scenarios that now preoccupy US defence planners is that they appear to assume actions incompatible with the modern Chinese way of war. Most Western analysts believe that, since 1949, China has used force largely for defensive and demonstrative purposes. Beijing's preferred mode of operation has been to launch sudden and stunning, but still limited, attacks. These are designed to get the enemy's attention and, by altering its assessment of the risks of persisting in behaviour that runs counter to Chinese interests, persuade it to change course. Beijing's brief but bloody war with Vietnam in 1979, its 1962 clash with India and its various military gestures in the South China Sea and across the Taiwan Strait are generally seen as illustrations of this tendency.[12]

Far from being inherently incompatible with such an approach, however, China's emerging A2/AD capabilities could actually fit quite comfortably within it. Using a handful of ballistic or cruise missiles to sink an enemy combatant (or even, as some Chinese military writers have suggested, firing a few missiles into the path of an oncoming US aircraft carrier) would send a swift and powerful signal of Beijing's resolve.[13] Unleashing a full-scale assault on US and/or allied bases and forces throughout the Western Pacific, as called for by the doctrine of 'Active Strategic Counterattacks on Exterior Lines', would obviously be another matter. The intent of such an attack might be familiar in certain respects: to bloody the enemy's nose and knock him back on his heels, in effect daring him to continue the fight. But the scale of the operation and the risk of escalation would make it more similar to China's entry into the Korean War than to even the most aggressive of the other actions Beijing has taken since 1950.

A coordinated attack designed to cripple the American military position in East Asia would be unlike anything the PLA has ever attempted before. Indeed, the closest analogue to such an operation would probably be the Japanese attack on Pearl Harbor and the accompanying offensives in Southeast Asia. Some Western analysts have suggested that Beijing might seek to replicate Japan's achievements in the first six months of the Pacific War, effectively kicking the US out of the Western Pacific, before hunkering down and daring it to fight its way back in. This scenario is best described by Jan van Tol:

> The PLA may be planning to conduct large-scale preemptive attacks designed to inflict severe damage on ... US forces based or operating forward; keep other US air and naval forces well out of range or unable to penetrate into the homeland; disrupt US command and control (C2) networks; and heavily constrain US operational logistics by destroying major supply nodes and the relatively few US logistics ships. The overall strategy may be to inflict substantial losses on US forces, lengthen US operational time-lines and highlight the United States' inability to

defend its allies. Once this is accomplished, the PLA could assume the strategic defense and deny reinforcing US forces access to the theater until the United States determines that it would be too costly to undo what would in effect be a *fait accompli*. In essence, this mimics the Imperial Japanese strategy of 1941–1942.[14]

It is, of course, very difficult at this point to picture China's military and civilian leaders risking everything on such a 'cosmic roll of the dice'. That said, the comparison to Japan should still give pause. Although they had far more combat experience than the PLA does today, on 7 December 1941, the Imperial Japanese Army and Navy launched an offensive for which their previous actions arguably provided little guidance. Nevertheless, for many years prior to the decision to go to war, Japanese planners had been experimenting with weapons, tactics and concepts of operation, seeking plausible solutions to the strategic problems posed by the presence of American air and naval power in the Pacific. China's military is at an earlier stage in its development, but appears to have embarked on a similar search.

Two other parallels are worth noting: Japanese decision-makers knew they were taking a huge gamble when they ordered an attack on Pearl Harbor but they saw themselves as behaving defensively, responding to hostile and provocative acts that left them with little choice. A series of American embargoes on exports of critical materials, culminating in a July 1941 ban on exports of oil and gasoline, posed a real threat to the Japanese war effort. As tensions worsened, the likelihood of direct US military intervention also seemed to grow. Under the circumstances, Tokyo preferred to begin a war on its own terms rather than wait for the Americans to start one on theirs. Future US decision-makers who believe they can use

economic sanctions or energy embargoes to compel conces-
sions, while heading off a possible armed conflict, would
do well to consider how their actions may be interpreted in
Beijing. A Chinese conventional first strike, if one comes, may
well be an act of desperation rather than a coldly calculated
'bolt from the blue'.

The example of Pearl Harbor should also serve as a reminder
of the fact that, despite their respect for the capabilities and
technological prowess of the US military, enemies have repeatedly underestimated US political resolve. Japanese planners
were convinced that the American people lacked the martial
spirit and capacity for sacrifice necessary to sustain a costly and
protracted slog across the Pacific. If present trends continue,
Chinese analysts could come to believe that the US has, in
fact, entered into a period of irreversible relative decline in its
national power and, if confronted, would back down rather
than fight back.

American interests

Suppose that China is attempting to acquire the forces needed
to implement its doctrine. It does not necessarily follow that
it would be in the United States' best interests to respond by
intensifying its own efforts to redress the deteriorating balance
of power; to the contrary, attempting to do so might be unnecessary and even counterproductive. Some observers have
suggested that vigorous US action could 'lead to an arms race
with China, which could culminate in a nuclear war'.[15] The
problem with this argument is threefold: firstly, it ignores the
fact that an arms competition of sorts is already under way,
albeit one in which, until recently, China was clearly the more
active and committed competitor. Also, the notion that arms
races lead inevitably to war is dubious, as the history of the
Cold War rivalry between the US and the Soviet Union should

suggest.[16] Finally, the risks of action need to be weighed against the potential dangers of inaction. Failure by the US to respond in a timely and effective way to the growth of Chinese power could weaken deterrence and increase the likelihood of aggressive behaviour that might escalate to war, even if this was not what China's leaders initially intended.

There are other objections to a vigorous American response. If the US takes the lead in countering China's military build-up, it may discourage other countries with ample resources from doing more for their own defence. For this reason, some analysts believe that, instead of 'pivoting' towards Asia, Washington should be backing away, finally breaking its allies decades-old habits' of dependence and free-riding.[17]

There is an obvious danger here. If the US does less, Japan, India, South Korea, Australia, the Philippines and Vietnam may feel the need to do more. However, each country faces a unique mix of fiscal, diplomatic and domestic political constraints that could mute or delay its balancing efforts. Without substantial help from the US, China's neighbours will have to pool their resources and cooperate more closely if they are to offset its growing strength. In the absence of strong American leadership, however, it may be harder for this disparate group of nations to coordinate their policies and easier for Beijing to drive wedges between them.

Weaker states sometimes seek to preserve their interests and guarantee their survival by appeasing rising powers or joining with them as junior partners. Some observers have even suggested that in Asia, unlike in Europe, bandwagoning has historically been more common than balancing. If China's power continues to grow, the region may be headed back to the future; not to a ceaseless struggle among contending states, as in eighteenth- and nineteenth-century Europe, but to a hierarchical (and relatively peaceful) Sino-centric regional order.[18]

Rather than attempting to oppose this trend, Americans might be better advised to learn to live with it.

Whether the US should give way gracefully and cede its place as Asia's predominant power is a question of vital strategic importance. A decision to move in this direction is extremely unlikely in the foreseeable future, if only because it would represent the abandonment of a goal that has been axiomatic to American foreign policy since the early part of the twentieth century. Under Republican and Democratic administrations alike, the US has worked (and sometimes fought) to prevent the domination of either Europe or Asia by a hostile power or coalition. This commitment has been rooted in a widely shared belief that, if either region fell under the sway of unfriendly forces, the US could find itself denied access to markets and vital resources. A regional hegemon might also be able to draw on the wealth and military capabilities of its neighbours to challenge US interests elsewhere in the world. American strategists have also long been concerned about the implications for their visions of a freer world if Europe or Asia was 'lost' to anti-democratic forces.[19]

Should China some day become a liberal democracy, the US would probably accept it as the preponderant player in East Asia. Until then, American policymakers will persist in their military and diplomatic efforts to maintain a favourable balance of power in the region. The success of this endeavour is by no means preordained, but, without a credible military strategy to counter China's increasing strength, it seems certain to fail.

Obstacles

The debate over the shape and substance of that strategy is still in its early days, having begun only after the US Department of Defense's (DoD) November 2011 announcement of the creation of an Air–Sea Battle Office (ASBO). The ASBO's stated mission is to guide the development of operational plans and the acquisition of capabilities that will, in the words of one DoD briefer, 'enable [US] forces to remain in a very challenging, a very complex A2/AD environment', staying 'right where they are' rather than being 'forced to move out'.[20]

While US officials have gone to considerable lengths to make the point that the ASBO's activities are not aimed at any one country, they are clearly directed, above all, at China. Twenty years after the First Gulf War caused Chinese strategists to focus their energies on a possible war with the US, their American counterparts are now beginning to engage in a similar collective exercise. Why did it take so long for this to happen?

It is not the case, of course, that prior to 2011 the US government simply ignored China's growing strength. To the contrary, since at least the mid-1990s, parts of the intelligence community have been intently focused on China. The military has maintained and updated its plans for various contingencies, in particular a possible conflict over Taiwan. For the past decade, decisions about basing, forward deployments, weapons acquisition and research and development (R&D) programmes have also been shaped, at least in part, by the prospect of intensifying competition and possible conflict with China. As will be discussed in Chapter Four, the creation of the ASBO came two years after a memorandum from the secretary of defence requesting the development of a new operational concept for addressing the A2/AD challenge. That request, in turn, grew out of deliberations extending back to the George W. Bush administration. But these disparate activities are different in breadth and intensity from the strategic debate that is now under way.

The United States' belated response to the Chinese military build-up is the result of a confluence of many factors.

Despite the resources devoted to studying it, China remains a notoriously hard intelligence target. Difficulty in obtaining reliable information about the PLA's plans and R&D activities is undoubtedly one reason why the US government has underestimated the pace and scope of its military programmes. Given China's heavy initial reliance on weapons imported from Russia, American analysts may also have been slow to appreciate its growing capacity for innovation and domestic production. In a remarkably candid acknowledgement of intelligence shortfalls, if not outright failures, in October 2009 Commander of US Pacific Command Admiral Robert F. Willard told reporters that, 'in the past decade or so, China has exceeded most of our intelligence estimates of their military capability and capacity, every year ... They've grown at an unprecedented rate in those capabilities.'[21] Although Willard did not elaborate, his comment suggests that the US intelligence community has been surprised by the early appearance of some weapons systems, and by the rate at which others have been produced and deployed.

In part because some of the 'dots' in Chinese military strategy have been slow to come into focus, American strategists have been slow to connect them and to appreciate their significance. This delay owes something to the fact that the pattern they form is an unfamiliar one. As Thomas Mahnken has pointed out, intelligence organisations often have difficulty in recognising substantial military innovations or 'new ways of war'. This tendency is the product of 'preconceptions about the character and conduct of war, ethnocentrism, and incomplete information'. Analysts are more likely to 'monitor the development of established weapons than to search for new military systems. It is also easier for them to detect technology and doctrine that have been demonstrated in war than weapons and concepts that have not seen combat.' In addition, especially in militaries that are accustomed to superiority, 'observers often pay greater attention to innovations in areas that their own services are exploring than to those that they have not examined, are not interested in, or have rejected.'[22]

As Mahnken suggests, these tendencies are all evident in the initial US reaction to the PLA's emerging A2/AD doctrine and capabilities, and especially its attempts to develop new types of weapons, such as an anti-ship ballistic missile. While some important parts of the programmes put in place, beginning in the 1990s, were carefully hidden from view, others, including the discussion of weapons and operational concepts for countering US power projection outlined in the previous chapter, were hiding in plain sight. Yet there was clearly a substantial lag between these first indications and a full appreciation of their significance. This gap cannot be attributed to a simple lack of information.

Most American observers took the lopsided outcome of the First Gulf War as proof of their country's unparalleled military preponderance and, in particular, its ability to bring air power to bear with devastating accuracy. In the prevailing climate of triumphalism, only a relative handful of analysts (many of them associated with the Pentagon's Office of Net Assessment and its director, Andrew Marshall) were prepared to take the next step, imagining a world in which other countries might soon acquire their own long-range, precision-strike systems. Against an adversary armed with such weapons, the US might no longer have the luxury of secure forward bases from which to prepare and launch an attack.[23]

The possibility that other states might seek to implement what came to be referred to as anti-access/area-denial strategies received only a brief mention in the 1997 National Defense Panel report, an independently authored document published in conjunction with the Pentagon's Quadrennial

Defense Review (QDR).[24] Four years later, however, the A2/ AD challenge was discussed in detail, and with a thinly veiled emphasis on China. In the near future, warned the 2001 QDR report, 'a military competitor with a formidable resource base' might emerge in Asia. Taking advantage of its proximity to the theatre of operations, this unnamed nation could buy large numbers of relatively inexpensive weapons capable of striking targets at comparatively modest distances from its own shores. These might not be as sophisticated as their American counterparts in every respect, but they could still be used to threaten ships at sea and to strike the handful of bases and facilities on which the US depended to sustain its forces in East Asia. If it played its cards right, a technologically inferior opponent might be able to neutralise the United States' overwhelming advantages in global power projection.[25]

In its treatment of the A2/AD challenge, the 2001 QDR clearly reflected the thinking of the Office of Net Assessment, whose director had worked for Donald Rumsfeld during his first stint as defence secretary in the late 1970s.[26] The document was well ahead of the armed services in this regard. Still, if not for unforeseen events, it would probably have served as the blueprint for Rumsfeld's plans to transform the American military and reorient it towards the Pacific. An original draft of the report, essentially complete before the 9/11 attacks, was delayed pending some hasty revisions that gave greater prominence to the newly relevant danger of mass-casualty terrorism. From that point on, the 'global war on terror' got first call on resources, and the attention of defence planners shifted from a hypothetical, high-intensity conflict in Asia with air and naval forces to two very real, ongoing counter-insurgencies, waged primarily on the ground in Afghanistan and Iraq.

Without 9/11, the US would doubtlessly have responded more adroitly to China's growing power. There were other causes for the delay, however, which had no direct relationship with Washington's newfound preoccupation with terrorism. In the popular imagination, military planners are always eagerly scanning the horizon in search of new threats to justify bigger budgets.[27] In the case of China, by contrast, there appears to have been a widespread reluctance to acknowledge an increasingly obvious challenge. This may have been due in part to an awareness that, if the doomsayers were right about the PLA's growing capabilities, the services would have had to respond in ways that would be deeply unsettling to existing plans and programmes. A shift in emphasis from counter-insurgency to high-intensity conventional conflict would obviously result in a reduced emphasis on ground forces, in favour of air and naval forces. But the implications for those services were also troubling, potentially requiring greater emphasis on longer-range aircraft at the cost of additional investment in tactical aviation, and placing carrier air power at increased risk.

Each of the military services thus had its own reasons for downplaying the threat or casting it into the indefinite future. These inclinations were reinforced by a more general lack of willingness to face up to the prospect of a possible conflict with China that persists in some quarters to the present day. Since the 1990s, American civilian and defence officials have been extremely careful about publicly identifying China as a potential military opponent. This caution is due in part to an understandable desire to avoid appearing unduly belligerent or hostile towards Beijing. US leaders recognised early on that there was nothing to be gained from such an attitude, either in their bilateral relations with China or in dealings with regional friends and allies fearful of a new Cold War.

But official circumspection has always reflected something deeper than mere diplomatic politesse. With few exceptions, the thinking of US politicians and, to a surprising extent, top military commanders has been influenced by the axiom that 'if we treat China like an enemy, it will become one.' First formulated in the 1990s by Joseph Nye, then assistant secretary of defence, this slogan has been repeated innumerable times since, in one form or another, by eminent personalities, including former defence secretaries and US Marine Corps generals.[28] The pervasiveness of this trope has obviously distorted the public discussion of alternative military strategies, forcing officials into awkward circumlocutions and barely credible denials. Such self-imposed restraint is not without consequences. Unless it can clearly identify and explain threats, a democratic government cannot hope to sustain popular support for the expenditures needed to address them. Nor is this merely a matter of public posturing. Anxiety about leaks can inhibit internal deliberations and planning exercises that cast China as a possible foe. Fear of making China an enemy has evidently discouraged thinking about what to do if, regardless of how it is treated, it nevertheless becomes one.

A final, powerful source of constraint is financial. In 2001, American strategists were just beginning to focus seriously on the long-term challenge from China when their attention was deflected by the more pressing problem of terrorism. After 9/11, money flowed freely to the DoD and intelligence agencies, but counter-terrorism and counter-insurgency were the top priorities. As the wars in Afghanistan and Iraq began to wind down, and as evidence of China's growing capabilities continued to accumulate, defence planners prepared to shift their attention from the Persian Gulf and Southwest Asia to the Western Pacific. It was precisely at this moment that a second 'black swan' – an unforeseen event with disproportionate consequences – occurred to again alter the course of history.

The global financial crisis that erupted in September 2008 caused growth rates to plummet, while budget deficits, debt and unemployment all rose to near-record peacetime levels. The lingering effects of the crisis have imposed powerful downward pressure on military spending and seem likely to continue to do so for the remainder of this decade, and perhaps beyond. Defence budgets would have been cut in any event as the US drew down its forces in Afghanistan and Iraq.

But the need to narrow deficits and reduce debt to something approximating pre-crisis levels, and the seeming inability of the two American political parties to agree on the best methods for doing so, have put the Pentagon on a path that points toward much deeper and more wide-ranging reductions than were anticipated only a few years ago. Even if draconian cuts can be avoided, the armed forces are going to have to make do with less. Responding to China's strategic challenge was never going to be easy; tight financial constraints will make it even tougher than it might otherwise have been.

Criteria

There are four criteria by which the various alternative approaches to this problem can be evaluated and compared. These are suggested by the specific challenges identified at the start of this chapter.

Deterrence and crisis stability

The first thing to ask about any proposed strategy is exactly how, and how effectively, it will deter China from attempting to use its growing capabilities to coerce or attack the US or its allies. The importance of these questions follows from the obvious desirability of avoiding war, as well as from the broader aims of American grand strategy. As it has done for over a century, the US seeks to prevent the domination of East Asia by a hostile power or coalition. In the longer run, it hopes to create conditions that may encourage China's peaceful transition towards liberal democracy. The preservation of a balance of power favourable to the US and its regional allies is essential to achieving these aims. In turn, maintaining a favourable balance requires developing capabilities and plans sufficient to persuade China's leaders that, by whatever methods of assessment they employ, it would not be in their interest to threaten or initiate the use of force.

The best deterrent is one that continues to function, even in the depths of a severe crisis, discouraging the transition from peace to war. All things being equal, American planners should prefer a strategy that reinforces crisis stability. In other words, to the extent that such a course is feasible, they should design a posture and a doctrine that neither tempt Chinese decision-makers with the prospect of a quick victory nor increase the likelihood that they will feel compelled to strike first for fear of defeat.

War fighting and escalation control

If deterrence fails, the US, most likely acting in concert with one or more of its regional allies, will use force in an attempt to achieve its operational and broader strategic goals. Any alternative strategy would need to be assessed by its objectives and by the 'theory of victory' that would link military means with desired political ends. The possible costs and risks of a proposed strategy also demand attention. In a collision between the US and China, one obvious concern would be the possibility of an escalation of violence and, in particular, from conventional to nuclear warfare.

Largely because of the dangers of escalation, Washington is unlikely to pursue maximal aims, such as unconditional surrender or the overthrow of the CCP regime. At the other end of the spectrum, the US could conceivably frame its goals in almost exclusively defensive terms: fending off an attack, restoring the *status quo ante* and bringing hostilities to a close at the earliest opportunity. However, if a rapid reversion to the status quo is impossible, or if achieving it would not be enough to bring the fighting to a halt, the US and its allies would likely pursue other, more aggressive options: using military operations to inflict pain and apply pressure sufficient to persuade Beijing to accept something that more closely resembles Washington's preferred terms, even as China, for its part, attempts to do the same.

Long-term competition

A third set of issues involves the likely impact of a proposed strategy on the long-term peacetime military competition. Especially in light of current unfavourable trends, the US must try to make decisions about force posture and doctrine that can help ease that competition in directions that benefit itself and its allies, while imposing disproportionate burdens on China. To the extent that it is possible, American and allied planners should attempt to modulate their own behaviour in order to elicit the desired reactions from their Chinese counterparts. The goals of this aspect of US strategy would be to encourage China to deploy weapons and adopt strategies that are less threatening to the US and its allies, and/or to impose greater economic burdens on China.

The ideal strategic manoeuvre would use low-cost actions (or perhaps even costless words) to induce an opponent to divert a substantial portion of its military budget from offensive to purely defensive weapons. Better yet would be a series of sequential moves that forced the enemy to scrap existing systems in order to field new ones at even greater expense. Such a dynamic approach could also help to strengthen and sustain deterrence by periodically reducing an opponent's confidence in its own capabilities.[29]

Reassurance

The final standard for evaluating a proposed strategy is whether it has the desired impact on allied or friendly governments and publics. Even as it seeks to deter potential opponents, in most situations, Washington is also working to reassure friends about its capabilities and intentions. Reassurance, in turn, serves several subsidiary purposes. Credible evidence of an American commitment can help persuade allies to maintain their ties to the US, thereby preventing them from slipping into neutrality or potentially being drawn into the camp of a hostile power. Keeping friendly countries on side is especially important in Asia, where the ability of the US to project military power is heavily dependent on access to local bases and facilities. Too much reassurance, however, can create a free-rider problem and increase the burdens borne by the US.

Washington, for example, tries to shape the defence policies of friendly governments through the security guarantees it extends. This typically requires striking a balance between doing too little and doing too much. American policymakers want to reassure allies sufficiently to discourage them from doing things (such as acquiring nuclear weapons) that the US regards as unnecessary or even dangerous, while at the same time encouraging them to take steps (such as increasing their defence budgets) that would contribute to the maintenance of a favourable regional power balance.

While each of these four criteria is important, there will inevitably be tensions among them. If they are perceived as being likely to impose minimal punishment for potential aggression, war-fighting strategies designed to deny an enemy success in achieving objectives through defensive operations alone may not be the best deterrents. Conversely, a strategy that relies on the threat of massive, or obviously dangerous, retaliation may be a good deterrent most of the time, but may not provide a sensible guide to actually fighting a war, should deterrence fail. Similarly, threatening certain actions may make sense if doing so provokes the desired response from a competitor in peacetime; actually executing those same threats in a crisis or a war may be another matter. Also, policies designed to reassure allies and deter opponents, such as the forward deployment of visible tokens of commitment, may create serious vulnerabilities in the event of war. In the real world, no one approach will meet all four criteria equally well, and designing a strategy will require trade-offs between multiple objectives.

Notes

1 For a good introduction to the concept and its application during the Cold War and after, see Thomas G. Mahnken (ed.), *Competitive Strategies for the 21st Century: Theory, History, and Practice* (Stanford, CA: Stanford University Press, 2012).

2 Robert S. Ross, 'The Problem With the Pivot', *Foreign Affairs*, vol. 91, no. 6, November–December 2012, p. 73.

3 For useful recent surveys, see Andrew S. Erickson, 'China's Modernization of Its Naval and Air Power Capabilities', in Ashley J. Tellis and Travis Tanner (eds), *China's Military Challenge* (Seattle, WA: National Bureau of Asian Research, 2012), pp. 61–126; and Mark A. Stokes, 'The Second Artillery Force and the Future of Long-Range Precision Strike', in *Ibid.*, pp. 127–62.

4 See Eric Hagt and Matthew Durnin, 'Space, China's Tactical Frontier', *Journal of Strategic Studies*, vol. 34, no. 5, October 2011, pp. 733–61. Hagt and Durnin suggest that the PLA may be able to do more with existing satellites than Western analysts expect by altering their orbits, tilting them or adjusting the angle of their sensors so as to expand the area they cover, and commandeering platforms intended primarily for civilian purposes to assist in military missions.

5 Andrew S. Erickson and David D. Yang, 'On the Verge of a Game-Changer', *US Naval Institute Proceedings*, vol. 135, 5/1,275, May 2009, pp. 27–32.

6 Garrett R. Wood, 'Offshore Control: A Rebuttal', *Infinity Journal*, 26 October 2012, https://www.infinityjournal.com/article.77/Offshore_Control_A_Rebuttal/.

7 The classic study on this topic is Paul Kennedy, *Rise of the Anglo-German Antagonism 1860–1914* (London: George Allen and Unwin, 1980).

8 See M. Taylor Fravel and Evan S. Medeiros, 'China's Search for Assured Retaliation', *International Security*, vol. 35, no. 2, Autumn 2010, pp. 48–87.

9 For a version of this argument, see Thomas J. Christensen, 'The Meaning of the Nuclear Evolution: China's Strategic Modernization and US-China Security Relations', *Journal of Strategic Studies,* vol. 35, no. 4, August 2012, pp. 447–87.

10 See Susan L. Shirk, *China: Fragile Superpower* (New York: Oxford University Press, 2007).

11 This argument is developed at length in H.E. Goemans, *War and Punishment: The Causes of War Termination and the First World War* (Princeton, NJ: Princeton University Press, 2000).

12 For overviews of this topic, see Allen S. Whiting, *The Chinese Calculus of Deterrence: India and Indochina* (Ann Arbor, MI: University of Michigan Press, 1975); Allen S. Whiting, *China Crosses the Yalu: Decision to Enter the Korean War* (New York: Macmillan, 1960); Allen S. Whiting, 'China's Use of Force, 1950–96, and Taiwan', *International Security,* vol. 26, no. 2, Autumn 2001, pp. 103–31; and Andrew Scobell, *China's Use of Military Force: Beyond the Great Wall and the Long March* (New York: Cambridge University Press, 2003).

13 On the possible utility of a 'proximity aircraft carrier deterrence' strike, which would launch missiles 'toward ... the front of the aircraft carrier battle group' to 'demonstrate one's ability and resolve', see Zhao Xijun (ed.), *Intimidation Warfare: A Comprehensive Discussion on Missile Deterrence* (Beijing: National Defense University Press, 2005), p. 192.

14 Jan van Tol et al., *AirSea Battle: A Point-of-Departure Operational Concept* (Washington DC: Center for Strategic and Budgetary Assessments, 2010), pp. 20–1.

15 Amitai Etzioni, 'Who Authorized Preparations for War with China?', *Yale Journal of International Affairs,* Summer 2013, pp. 37–51.

16 This does not mean that an intensifying arms competition between the US and China would be a good thing or that efforts to constrain it are not worth considering. For a discussion of the prospects for arms control, see Conclusion.

17 See Justin Logan, 'China, America, and the Pivot to Asia', *Policy Analysis,* no. 717, 8 January 2013. For a general statement of the case for what is sometimes referred to as a strategy of 'offshore balancing', see Christopher Layne, 'From Preponderance to Offshore Balancing: America's Future Grand Strategy', *International Security,* vol. 22, no. 1, Summer 1997, pp. 86–124.

18 Samuel P. Huntington, *The Clash of Civilizations and the Remaking of World Order* (New York: Simon and Schuster, 1996), p. 234. For an elaboration of this argument, see David C. Kang, *China Rising: Peace, Power, and Order in East Asia* (New York: Columbia University Press, 2007).

19 This section draws on Aaron L. Friedberg, *A Contest for Supremacy: China, America and the Struggle for Mastery in Asia* (New York: W.W. Norton & Company, 2011), p. 7.

20 DoD, 'Background Briefing on Air-Sea Battle by Defense Officials from the Pentagon', 9 November 2011, http://www.defense.gov/transcripts/transcript.aspx?transcriptid=4923.

21 See Thomas G. Mahnken, 'China's Anti-Access Strategy in Historical and Theoretical Perspective', *Journal of Strategic Studies*, vol. 34, no. 3, June 2011, pp. 299–323.

22 *Ibid.*, p. 302.

23 For overviews of this topic, see Andrew Krepinevich, Barry Watts and Robert Work, *Meeting the Anti-Access and Area-Denial Challenge* (Washington DC: Center for Strategic and Budgetary Assessments, 2003); and Barry Watts, *The Maturing Revolution in Military Affairs* (Washington DC: Center for Strategic and Budgetary Assessments, 2011).

24 National Defense Panel, *Transforming Defense: National Security in the 21st Century*, December 1997, http://www.fas. org/man/docs/ndp/part01.htm.

25 US Department of Defense, *Quadrennial Defense Review Report*, 30 September 2001, p. 4, http:// www.defense.gov/pubs/pdfs/ qdr2001.pdf.

26 See Thomas E. Ricks, 'Rumsfeld Outlines Defense Overhaul', *Washington Post*, 23 March 2001; Michael R. Gordon, 'Pentagon Review Puts Emphasis on Long-Range Arms in Pacific', *New York Times*, 17 May 2001, http://www. nytimes.com/2001/05/17/world/ pentagon-review-puts-emphasis- on-long-range-arms-in-pacific. html; and Nicholas Lemann, 'Dreaming About War', *New Yorker*, 16 July 2001, http://www.comw. org/qdr/0107lemann.html.

27 See, for example, Etzioni, 'Who Authorized Preparations for War With China?', pp. 37–51.

28 Joseph Nye, Jr, 'The Case Against Containment: Treat China Like an Enemy and That's What It Will Be', *Global Beat*, 22 June 1998. According to former defence secretary Robert Gates, 'if we treat China like an enemy, it will become one.' 'Robert Gates Speaks at OSU', *Daily Collegian*, 24 October 2012. In a variation on this theme, the former vice chairman of the US Joint Chiefs of Staff, General James Cartwright, warned that discussion of Air–Sea Battle doctrine was 'demonizing China. That's not in anybody's interest.' Sydney J. Freedberg, Jr, 'Cartwright Targets F-35, AirSea Battle; Warns of $250B More Cuts', *Breaking Defense*, 15 May 2012, http:// breakingdefense.com/2012/05/15/ cartwright-savages-f-35-airsea- battle-warns-of-250-billion-mo/. The fact that both Gates and Cartwright were speaking as former officials suggests that they were expressing their genuine beliefs rather than merely mouthing talking points.

29 For several attempts to apply a competitive-strategies approach to China, see Mahnken (ed.), *Competitive Strategies for the 21st Century*.

CHAPTER THREE

The direct approach: Air–Sea Battle

There are, at present, two broad schools of thought regarding the future of American military strategy in Asia. On one side are the advocates of what might be called the direct approach. Analysts and officials in this camp argue that, in the event of hostilities, the United States would have no choice but to defeat and disable China's anti-access/area-denial (A2/AD) capabilities using a variety of offensive and defensive means, including conventional strikes against targets on the Chinese mainland. Those who take this view have generally rallied around the so-called Air–Sea Battle (ASB) concept.

Largely in response to ASB's perceived dangers and inadequacies, a number of analysts have proposed that the US and its allies instead adopt some kind of indirect response to China's growing military power. While several alternatives have been advanced, all eschew direct attacks on Chinese territory, instead primarily depending on the application of American and allied naval power to bring Beijing to terms. Indirect strategies can be subdivided into two groups. Some seek to avoid China's anti-access capabilities altogether by imposing a distant blockade, interdicting ships (especially those carrying oil and natural gas) at geographical choke points far removed from its territory. Other, more aggressive maritime-denial strategies call for the US and its allies to use their undersea warfare capabilities to mine harbours, sink ships and prevent China from using even its coastal waters.

Concept

In the last five years, the question of how to preserve Washington's ability to project military power has risen to become one of the Pentagon's top strategic priorities. In its 2012 list of ten 'primary missions', the US Department of Defense (DoD) ranked the ability to 'project power despite anti-access/area denial challenges' third, behind only 'counter terrorism and irregular warfare' and the ability to 'deter and defeat aggression'.[1] Officials have been at pains to point out that the proliferation of A2/AD capabilities is a general trend, and to avoid publicly identifying any one country as the most likely foe. Nevertheless, it is evident that China's emerging capabilities are the single most important source of concern and the driving force behind the search for solutions to the anti-access challenge.

In July 2009, Robert Gates, then defence secretary, instructed military planners to explore options to 'preserve US ability to project power and maintain freedom of action in the global commons'.[2] Six months later, the 2010 Quadrennial Defense Review reported that: 'the Air Force and Navy together are developing a new joint air-sea battle concept for defeating … adversaries equipped with sophisticated anti-access and area denial capabilities.'[3] This announcement was followed, in November 2011, by the circulation of a so-called Joint Operational Access Concept (JOAC), a cross-service document meant, in the words of Chairman of the Joint Chiefs of Staff Martin Dempsey, to describe 'in broad terms my vision for how joint forces will operate in response to emerging anti-access and area-denial security challenges'.[4] The circulation of the JOAC was accompanied by the creation of a joint Air–Sea Battle Office (ASBO) of the air force and navy, charged with overseeing the further refinement and implementation of a concept that 'integrates air and naval forces in order to operate in the antiaccess area-denial environment'.[5]

Since its unveiling in late 2011, several high-ranking officials have made statements intended to clarify the significance and limitations of the ASBO's work. In part because of the controversy and confusion that have surrounded it, in May 2013, the DoD published an unclassified summary of the ASB concept. While the most recent statements are somewhat more concrete and detailed, they stop well short of providing details regarding the weapons and tactics with which the military would wage an ASB campaign. This discretion is due to diplomatic delicacy and obvious concerns about secrecy, but also reflects the fact that ASB remains a work in progress.

In a series of speeches and articles, Norton Schwartz, then air-force chief of staff, and Chief of Naval Operations Admiral Jonathan Greenert described ASB as a response to a broad, emerging challenge rather than a specific, imminent threat. In the two decades since the collapse of the Soviet Union, notes Schwartz, 'our ability to project expeditionary power from the United States, our access to forward bases, and our mobility throughout potential battle spaces has remained largely unchallenged.' Today, however, 'this advantage is being threatened.'[6]

At the deepest level, the challenge is a manifestation of the ongoing 'proliferation of advanced technology and computing power'.[7] Particularly concerning, according to Schwartz and Greenert, 'is the sustained effort by certain states to develop, stockpile and proliferate advanced long-range precision weapons ... networked and integrated with sophisticated over-the-horizon surveillance systems'. The outer edge of the 'anti-access envelope' is being extended still further in some cases by 'growing fleets of diesel submarines, improved fighter and bomber aircraft, and surface combatants with advanced air defense and electronic warfare systems'. Taken together, these capabilities may enable 'rising powers that appear to be seeking regional hegemony' to 'isolate other regional actors from American military intervention', thereby 'enabling them to more effectively intimidate and coerce neighboring states'.[8] A suitably armed hostile power could 'drive allies and partners to seek accommodation ... or to develop alternate means of self-defense with potentially destabilizing effects'.[9]

Challenges to Washington's ability to project its military power across transoceanic distances are nothing new. Indeed, in retrospect, the brief interval of unimpeded global access appears to have been a historical anomaly. As the DoD's JOAC document makes clear, 'the contest over operational access can dominate practically all other considerations in warfare, as it did throughout the Pacific theater and in the battle for the North Atlantic during the Second World War.' In a future conflict against a sophisticated opponent, the American military may once again be given the task of 'gaining and maintaining operational access in the face of armed opposition'.[10]

In light of growing threats, the US needs to devise plans and acquire capabilities that will enable it to 'maintain [its] ability to project power in areas in which [its] access and freedom to operate are challenged'.[11] But how can this be achieved? The JOAC presents a list of 11 'operational access precepts', the first of which is that US forces must 'leverage cross-domain synergy', using 'airpower to defeat antiship weapons, naval power to neutralize air defenses, ground forces to neutralize land-based threats to air and naval forces, cyber operations to defeat space systems and so on'.[12] Some of the other proposed measures are defensive in character – for example, considering a variety of basing options and maximising surprise through 'deception, stealth, and ambiguity to complicate enemy targeting' – but most have a distinctly offensive tone. Among these are recommendations that US forces 'disrupt enemy reconnaissance and surveillance efforts while protecting friendly efforts'; 'protect space and cyber assets while attacking the enemy's space and cyber capabilities'; and 'attack enemy anti-access/area-denial defense in depth rather than rolling back those defenses from the perimeter'.[13]

The 2013 unclassified ASB concept paper provides further details about the specific nature of the threat and a description of the main themes of a US response. The paper begins with what are described as conservative and realistic assumptions regarding how an enemy would use its A2/AD capabilities. To begin with, it is assumed that 'the adversary will initiate military activities with little or no ... warning'. As a result, 'forward friendly forces will be in an A2/AD environment at the commencement of hostilities', and must be prepared to offer 'an immediate and effective response'. Because such strikes are crucial to its chances of success, a determined enemy will not hesitate to attack US bases on allied soil. Indeed, even the continental US would be susceptible to attack. As a result, 'the defense of all bases from which US forces operate must be addressed.' Echoing the JOAC's emphasis on the multiple domains of modern warfare, the concept paper also asserts that all five (space, cyberspace, air, maritime and land) 'will be contested by an adversary', and that none can be 'completely ceded' to it.[14]

According to its authors, 'the ASB Concept's solution to the A2/AD challenge ... is to develop networked, integrated forces capable of attack-in-depth to disrupt, destroy and defeat adversary forces (NIA/D3).'[15] Networking and integration are essential to enabling cross-domain operations of the sort envisioned in the JOAC.[16] 'Attack-in-depth' requires having the ability to 'project forces through denied ... zones' and applying 'both kinetic and non-kinetic means to address adversary critical vulnerabilities', without having first systematically destroyed and rolled back the enemy's air defences.[17]

At the heart of the ASB concept are three 'lines of effort'. US and allied forces will seek to 'disrupt' the enemy's command, control, computers, intelligence, surveillance and reconnaissance (C4ISR) capabilities, denying it the ability to track and locate targets and 'ideally precluding attack on friendly forces'. They will attempt to 'destroy' the adversary's A2/AD platforms and weapons systems, before at least some of them are used, thereby reducing its ability to launch strikes and enhancing 'friendly survivability', while providing greater 'freedom of action'. Finally, to the extent that the enemy succeeds in unleashing them, US and allied forces will aim to 'defeat' the opponent's weapons 'post-launch'.[18]

The chief of naval operations and the chief of staff of the air force have summed up the aim of the ASB concept, in characteristically blunt American military jargon, as being to break the enemy's 'kill chain'. They note that in order to carry out an attack, 'an adversary must complete a sequence of actions', locating US forces, relaying information, launching weapons and zeroing in on targets. 'Each of these steps is vulnerable to interdiction or disruption, and because each step must work, our forces can focus on the weakest links in the chain, not each and every one.'[19] While Greenert and Welsh do not say so, it seems clear that the weakest links are those at the top of the chain and involve C4ISR systems, without which effective enemy attacks would be impossible.

Government officials have assiduously avoided any discussion of how the ASB concept might be applied to China.[20]

The most detailed treatment of this question is a 2010 think-tank study by former US Navy captain Jan van Tol. While it undoubtedly deviates from current Pentagon thinking in some respects, van Tol's paper lays out several 'distinct lines of operation' that match up closely with those identified in the ASB concept paper. These include 'withstanding the initial attack and limiting damage to US and allied forces and bases; executing a blinding campaign against PLA battle networks'; and 'executing a suppression campaign against PLA long-range, principally strike systems'.[21] The second of these tasks is vital to achieving eventual victory. In van Tol's words, 'blinding PLA systems is essential for AirSea Battle's success in every other line of operation.'[22] Doing so requires prompt attacks, including kinetic strikes, on a range of critical targets, such as Chinese satellites, ground stations, counter-space capabilities and over-the-horizon radars. Hitting these radars should be, van Tol says, 'among the earliest US strike priorities'.[23]

Attacks on People's Liberation Army (PLA) land-based missiles would follow closely on the heels of the initial 'blinding' strikes, but would unfold over a longer period of time. After creating 'multi-axis corridors' by degrading Chinese air-defence systems, the US would use a combination of stand-off weapons (including cruise missiles fired from submarines) and penetrating systems (including stealthy manned bombers and unmanned drones) to locate and attack land-based missile launchers and their command-and-control networks. While 'the PLA's inventory of missiles and mobile launchers is too numerous and generally too difficult to find to realize a high level of destruction', missile-suppression operations could reduce the size and coordination of attacks against US and allied targets. Among other benefits, this would mean that allied missile-defence systems would have the easier task of coping with a 'drizzle' rather than a 'downpour' of incoming

PLA weapons. Van Tol concludes that success in destroying platforms and weapons systems is 'critical to preventing China from achieving a quick "knock-out" blow'.[24]

Assessment

There are two common criticisms of ASB: that it is nothing more than a justification for greater spending on air and naval forces at the expense of ground forces, and that it is not a fully developed strategy. Both claims contain an element of truth, but neither is a refutation of the concept. The enthusiasm for ASB shown by top air-force and navy officers is undoubtedly due, in part, to its relatively favourable implications for their services. Similarly, parochial motives are also partly responsible for the objections raised by some US Army and Marine Corps analysts, as well as the recent attempts by the leaders of these branches to define a role for ground forces within the new operational concept. These facts tell us little, however, about the origins of ASB and nothing at all about its potential utility.[25]

The observations of some critics that ASB is 'an operational concept looking for a strategy',[26] and that it lacks 'a theory of victory against China'[27] are, strictly speaking, correct. But these are not claims with which informed ASB advocates would disagree. Seeking to lay this critique to rest, the ASBO's May 2013 paper explicitly acknowledges that 'ASB is not a strategy'.[28] Instead, it is what the JOAC describes as 'a warfighting concept'; namely, a 'limited operational concept that focuses on the development of integrated air and naval forces in the context of antiaccess/area-denial threats'. Its purpose is to identify 'the actions needed to defeat those threats and the material and nonmaterial investments required to execute those actions'.[29] In other words, ASB is an outline or a general approach meant to guide planners in the solution of a particular operational problem.

As one defender of the concept notes, ASB does not purport to 'identify the ends desired and the risks inherent in a specific strategy'.[30] It tells planners how to 'kick in the door' but has nothing to say about what they should do next, if they succeed. In the words of one DoD spokesman, 'whatever it is that the combatant commander wants to achieve after that, that's entirely up to their discretion.'[31] At best, ASB can only be a component of a larger strategy that includes plans and preparations for linking the achievement of initial military objectives to what Clausewitz termed 'the political object of the war'.

War fighting

What would be the result of a Sino-American conflict in which the PLA employed the weapons and doctrine described in Chapter One, and the US sought to implement some variant of ASB? This question can be broken down into three parts: firstly, what would be the outcome, in strictly military terms, of a series of exchanges between the two forces? Secondly, how likely is it that these initial exchanges would yield a swift diplomatic resolution to any conflict? And, thirdly, what are the chances that they would lead instead to nuclear escalation?

Military outcomes

As the ASBO's unclassified paper makes clear, US planners assume that, if it ever comes, a Sino-American war will begin with a Chinese first strike. Much will therefore depend on how well the US and its allies can 'take a punch'. It is on precisely this point, however, that the growth of China's A2/AD capabilities has begun to cause grave doubts. As has already been suggested, without significant remedial measures, the ability of the US to defend its forward-deployed forces and bases by, as the ASBO's concept paper puts it, 'defeating' incoming Chinese weapons will continue to erode. Within the next 5–10 years, the PLA will be able to inflict significant damage on every one of the fixed installations on which the US presently relies to sustain its forces in the Western Pacific, including those as far east as Guam, assuming that China lands the first blow. The prospects for defending these fixed facilities through active measures alone do not appear to be promising. Barring a considerable increase in the size and effectiveness of existing, kinetic-kill anti-missile systems, China's Second Artillery Force will probably be able to overwhelm US and allied defences with massed attacks and decoys.[32] Using a mixture of ballistic missiles, cruise missiles and torpedoes, the PLA may also be able to sink some American surface vessels (including aircraft carriers) operating within 1,500 nautical miles off China's coast.

In addition to intercepting Chinese weapons before they reach their targets, the US and its allies can diminish their effectiveness through the use of passive–defensive techniques. If strategic warning is available, the impact of an initial strike could be reduced by dispersing aircraft to secondary airfields; putting all serviceable vessels to sea; implementing deception measures to conceal the location of planes and major naval combatants; and perhaps pulling some key assets back beyond the effective range of Chinese ballistic missiles. These manoeuvres might enable US and allied forces to continue fighting, but they would probably also diminish their ability to conduct coordinated early counter-attacks. If Chinese forces can revisit targets at will to conduct follow-on strikes (perhaps using manned aircraft, as well as missiles, once allied air defences have been degraded), they will have a good chance of retaining the initiative and blunting any response.

Even a very successful opening blow would not necessarily prevent the US from responding with a prompt blinding campaign aimed at disrupting China's C4ISR networks. This campaign could begin immediately after an attack had been detected and would be executed, in part, using virtually instantaneous means, including the jamming or disabling of orbiting satellites, and cyber and electronic-warfare (EW) attacks on enemy sensors and computer networks. Physical strikes on selected targets could be carried out with weapons fired from platforms that are either less vulnerable to pre-emption than surface ships and land-based aircraft, such as attack submarines, or not based within the theatre at all, such as stealthy, penetrating bombers.

Unless they are willing to rely entirely on cyber attacks and other non-kinetic measures, US planners will want to retain the capacity to strike key parts of China's C4ISR network using precision-guided conventional weapons. Given that some critical PLA facilities are located far inland, outside the range of current sea-launched cruise missiles, the success of a blinding campaign carried out in the relatively near term would therefore appear to be heavily dependent on the ability of stealthy manned aircraft to penetrate Chinese air defences. An unanticipated breakthrough in China's ability to track and target these planes, or an unexpected willingness to use unconventional tactics to disable them before they can leave the ground (perhaps by sabotaging their bases, including those in the continental US), could sharply reduce the effectiveness of an American blinding campaign.

The success of this campaign will have an impact on the ability of US forces to suppress follow-on attacks by destroying remaining Chinese weapons and platforms. The more complete the disruption of China's command-and-control networks, especially those associated with its air-defence system, the greater the freedom of action that US forces will subsequently enjoy. Still, given the array of targets involved and the possibilities for dispersal and concealment, this would be an extremely challenging mission and parts of it would be impossible with presently deployed forces.

Reducing China's ability to launch further attacks from maritime platforms should be relatively easy. US submarines could sink enemy surface ships and hunt submarines, as well as fire cruise missiles at targets with known locations on land. Assuming that blinding attacks had been successful, US carriers and other surface combatants could operate more safely off China's shores, helping to clear the waters of People's Liberation Army Navy (PLAN) stragglers and launching additional strikes on the mainland.

Stripping China of its ability to continue launching cruise and ballistic missiles from land would be another matter. Many of its most capable systems are mobile, its territory is vast and its military has long experience in cover, concealment, deception and hardening. The PLA would presumably have dispersed as many weapons as possible either before or immediately after unleashing its first strike, and US forces would have to find them before they could be destroyed.

As van Tol notes, American 'legacy bombers with precision-guided stand-off munitions' could attack 'known fixed missile emplacements' and other installations. But finding and destroying mobile missile launchers would require 'long-endurance manned and unmanned stealthy penetrators' of a sort that the US does not currently possess.[33] While the degradation of its C4ISR capabilities would make it much more difficult for the PLA to assess damage or locate US and allied mobile targets (especially ships at sea), it could still fire blind, launching weapons from pre-sited locations against fixed installations, such as ports and airfields.

Political outcomes

Regardless of which country did better in achieving its initial military objectives, neither the US nor China would likely have put itself in a position to dictate terms to the other. Those who point out that ASB alone does not contain a 'theory of victory' are correct; but neither does the Chinese concept of 'Active Strategic Counterattacks on Exterior Lines' (see Chapter One). Even if the PLA succeeded in inflicting terrible damage on US forward-based forces and facilities, unless it also launched devastating attacks on American territory, it would have done little to prevent its enemy from mobilising, regrouping and continuing the war. Nothing in the nation's history suggests that the US would respond to an initial defeat by suing for peace.

Similarly, wholly successful implementation of the ASB concept would diminish China's capacity to launch conventional strikes on US allies, forces and bases, and might clear the way for US and allied forces to conduct follow-on operations, such as the various types of blockade described in the next chapter. But even a humiliating defeat in the opening stages of a war might not be sufficient to cause Beijing to seek a prompt diplomatic settlement. To the contrary, it could cause China's leaders to conclude that they faced a choice between fighting on or losing their grip on domestic political power.

Nuclear escalation

Critics of ASB have far less to say about its effectiveness as an operational concept than about its alleged escalatory potential. Indeed, the charge most commonly levied against ASB is that conventional strikes on the Chinese mainland, of the sort the concept envisions, could provoke a nuclear response. Despite the fact that Beijing continues to proclaim its adherence to a doctrine of no first use, in recent years, Chinese analysts have suggested publicly that, in some instances, the PLA might be prepared to use nuclear weapons in retaliation to conventional attacks.[34] The purpose of such statements is presumably to bolster deterrence of non-nuclear strikes by raising doubts about the Chinese response. It may, therefore, be in Beijing's interest to issue such warnings. But how seriously should they be taken?

A successful Chinese conventional first strike would damage or destroy US bases on foreign soil (and, if it included attacks on Guam, on sovereign American territory as well), and would kill hundreds, perhaps thousands, of Americans. Unless Chinese strategists believed that their counterparts drew a sharp distinction between targets in the Western Pacific and those on the American mainland, they could hardly be shocked if the US retaliated by hitting some of the sites from which the attacks were launched. Whatever hints they may have dropped beforehand, it is unlikely that Chinese decision-makers would react reflexively or in a blind rage, resorting to the use of nuclear weapons in response to any attack on their territory.[35]

If the American arsenal of deployed long-range nuclear weapons continues to shrink while China's grows, the overall balance between them could shift in ways that would make the threat of escalation more credible.[36] Facing a reduced US force, and with an expanded and more secure second-strike force of their own, Chinese planners might believe that they could engage in limited nuclear attacks while deterring large-scale retaliation. For the moment, however, Beijing would have to fear that using nuclear weapons in response to American conventional attacks would provoke a devastating response. Given the relative size and survivability of the two nation's arsenals, a nuclear exchange would leave China far worse off than the US. Desperate, but still rational, leaders might be willing to gamble that a nuclear 'shot across the bow' with one or two weapons could shock the US into suspending attacks on Chinese territory, but they would also have to recognise that such a gesture could have fatal consequences for themselves and their regime.[37]

Whether as the result of a deliberate decision or a break-down in command and control, escalation could nevertheless be the unintended consequence of successful US strikes on key targets in China. If the Second Artillery Force based or stored conventional and nuclear missiles close to one another in some locations, it might appear that the Americans were trying to degrade or destroy China's retaliatory capabilities, even if this was not the case. Because their payloads would not be known until they reached their targets, the use of conventionally armed ballistic missiles by the US could make the problem even more acute. In addition to reducing China's ability to launch coordinated follow-on A2/AD attacks, a blinding campaign could also disrupt communications networks while depriving Beijing of early-warning radars and reconnaissance satellites. In such circumstances, China's leaders might believe that they faced a choice between using their nuclear forces or losing them. Even more frightening is the prospect that, in the confusion following an American conventional counter-attack, nuclear weapons could be launched inadvertently or without orders from the appropriate authorities.[38] While it is impossible to evaluate these risks with any degree of assurance, they cannot help but weigh heavily on the minds of American policymakers faced with the decision of whether to launch strikes on the Chinese mainland.

It is worth recalling that China's leaders also cannot be certain that their use of conventional weapons would not provoke a nuclear response from the US.

As things now stand, they have good reason to be concerned. Washington has never ruled out being the first to use nuclear weapons; to the contrary, its policy of extended deterrence has always left open the possibility that it might do so in response to conventional, as well as nuclear, attacks on its allies. The credibility of such threats may have been weakened by recent statements to the effect that the US intends to reduce its reliance on nuclear weapons and hopes eventually to eliminate them.[39] The reliability of US threats could be further eroded by the growing size and reduced vulnerability of China's long-range nuclear forces, as well as additional cuts in the American nuclear arsenal and Washington's adoption of a no-first-use doctrine. For the time being, however, Chinese planners still have reason to fear that a successful conventional first strike might provoke a nuclear response that would erase whatever gains they had made.

Deterrence

Compared to the question of ASB's impact on military outcomes, its contribution to deterrence has received relatively little attention. Defenders of the concept generally treat deterrent efficacy as an inevitable by-product of war-fighting effectiveness. In this view, if the US and its allies can defeat an anti-access campaign, China should be deterred from ever launching one. This simple proposition glosses over an important intervening process of assessment: even if its advocates are correct in their judgement about military outcomes, ASB will not work as a deterrent unless Chinese decision-makers come to similar conclusions. A serious estimate of the concept's contribution to deterrence therefore demands a deep understanding of how PLA planners measure the military balance and predict the likely outcome of a future war with the US.

That said, ASB has the potential to activate all three of the mechanisms identified by deterrence theorists: the promise of denial, the prospect of punishment and what Thomas Schelling called the 'threat that leaves something to chance'.[40] As they contemplate launching an A2/AD campaign, China's leaders could be discouraged by the belief that their initial attacks simply will not work, or that they will fail to achieve a level of damage high enough to cripple the United States' ability to project power into the Western Pacific. A combination of doubt over the performance of their own systems and a generous estimate of the effectiveness of US and allied active and passive defences might be enough to yield this conclusion.

The problem with a purely defensive strategy of deterrence through denial is that it may not pose sufficient risks to a potential aggressor. If there was no additional response from the US and its allies, those Chinese leaders who had ordered a failed A2/AD attack might experience a loss of face but, aside from the cost of the weapons used, would not incur any significant material loss. A conventional counter-offensive, of the sort envisioned under ASB, would change this calculus considerably. US retaliation could destroy critical portions of China's command-and-control network, along with missile storage, manufacturing and launch sites. Further salvoes might also damage ports, airfields, logistical hubs and perhaps parts of the domestic security apparatus, including facilities associated with the security services and the People's Armed Police Force.

Credibly threatening to defeat a first strike rather than merely repelling it, as well as destroying significant parts of China's military and security apparatus, would raise the anticipated costs of an attack, thereby presumably helping to deter such an assault.[41]

The danger of nuclear escalation associated with the offensive aspects of ASB can make an additional contribution to deterrence. Chinese decision-makers contemplating a conventional first strike may doubt that the US would respond with prompt nuclear retaliation. But for reasons already discussed, they would have cause to fear that, regardless of what anyone intends, their actions could set in train a series of events that would result in disaster for all concerned. If PLA planners believe that the US would respond to a first strike with a blinding campaign, and if they recognise that this could force them to contemplate using or losing their own nuclear weapons, their desire to avoid being put in such a situation might cause them to refrain from launching an A2/AD campaign in the first place. In short, those who warn of ASB's escalatory potential may be right; but this very fact could actually enhance its deterrent utility. Regardless of whether it would be wise for US decision-makers to launch prompt conventional counter-attacks on China's C4ISR networks, acquiring the capacity to do so could help make it less likely that they would ever have to make that decision.

In addition to the issue of escalation from conventional to nuclear war, there is the question of ASB's impact on crisis stability. A tense confrontation between opponents armed with highly capable, but potentially fragile, conventional precision-strike complexes could replicate the 'two scorpions in a bottle' problem (in which each side fears a disarming first strike by the other) that so troubled nuclear strategists during the Cold War.[42] If Chinese decision-makers fear that the US is about to launch a blinding attack that would drastically decrease the effectiveness of their A2/AD forces, they might feel compelled to start a war by striking first.

The US can mitigate this danger, to some degree, by reducing the vulnerability of its own weapons systems, information networks and C4ISR platforms, thereby minimising whatever advantage Beijing might hope to gain by initiating hostilities. Given the increasing reach and accuracy of Chinese forces, these are defensive steps that should be taken no matter what strategy the US adopts. The real question is whether the US should forgo enhancing its own offensive capabilities to avoid posing too great a threat to those of China. There is a chance that such unilateral self-restraint might, in some circumstances, reduce the risk of war. If deterrence fails, however, it would certainly leave the US with fewer options for conducting counter-attacks that could limit damage to its own forces and those of its allies.

Long-term competition
The impact of ASB on the ongoing Sino-American strategic competition will depend, in part, on how the concept is implemented. As has been suggested, because of the relatively low cost to China of acquiring still more ballistic missiles, trying to defend fixed facilities and ships by relying primarily on traditional kinetic-kill defence systems does not look like a winning proposition for the US and its allies. On the other hand, adding a mixture of hardening, dispersal and concealment could complicate the plans of an attacker at comparatively low cost, while enhancing the effectiveness of active defences, especially against a 'blind' opponent.[43]

A far higher pay-off would come from the development of effective directed-energy (DE) weapons. As one study notes, such systems 'could provide US forces with nearly unlimited magazines to counter incoming missiles at a negligible cost per shot', thereby reversing 'the cost-imposition calculus of future missile competitions in favor of the United States'.[44] The introduction of DE weapons could thus neutralise the centrepiece of China's A2/AD strategy and render obsolete systems that have taken decades, and many billions of dollars, to develop and refine. It remains to be seen whether such weapons can be used effectively on the battlefield, where they could face relatively inexpensive countermeasures, among other challenges.

There are also different ways to implement the offensive elements of ASB. Manned fighter-bombers (such as the F-35) do not appear to be the most effective means for delivering strikes against targets on the Chinese mainland, due to their restricted operational range, limited payloads, possible susceptibility to sophisticated integrated air-defence systems (IADS) and the potential vulnerability of the carriers and regional bases from which they would be launched. These platforms are also very expensive and could end up absorbing a disproportionate share of available resources.[45] Equipping attack submarines with a greater number of conventionally armed cruise missiles would provide a more reliable means for carrying out precision strikes in response to a Chinese attack. However, existing cruise missiles lack the range to hit targets deep inside China.[46]

A variety of other weapons that have not yet been developed or deployed could be used to carry out conventional strikes against facilities virtually anywhere in China, from beyond the reach of its A2/AD systems. These include: unmanned, carrier-launched strike aircraft (UCAS); conventionally armed, submarine-launched, intermediate-range ballistic missiles; a new manned, penetrating bomber; land-based conventional ballistic missiles (either a new type of intermediate-range missile or a conventionally armed intercontinental ballistic missile [ICBM]); and some kind of hypersonic 'prompt global strike' vehicle, capable of delivering conventional munitions against targets anywhere in the world, in under an hour, from bases in the US. Among these, few have advanced much beyond the concept-development phase. Also, the various possible conventional ballistic missiles are all controversial because of fears that their launch could be misinterpreted as the start of a pre-emptive nuclear attack.[47]

From a competitive-strategies perspective, there could be significant advantages for the US in retaining an air-breathing component to its long-range conventional precision-strike threat, while adding another dimension by deploying some kind of ballistic-missile delivery system. Since the early 1990s, PLA planners have sought to counter the potential of American 'smart' bombs and cruise missiles by taking the offensive: acquiring A2/AD systems to push US forces back beyond the range at which they can effectively use their precision-strike weapons. At the same time, however, China has spent vast sums on defensive measures: building an IADS, trying to find ways to counter American stealth technology and taking other costly steps (such as developing and deploying mobile ICBMs and building an extensive network of underground facilities), motivated, at least in part, by fear of a conventional attack. The resources expended on these projects might otherwise have gone towards further strengthening China's offensive capabilities.

Preserving and, if possible at a reasonable cost, enhancing the ability to threaten critical targets with aircraft and cruise missiles would reinforce China's existing inclination to invest in active and passive defences against air-breathing, aerial attack.[48] Simultaneously developing, and perhaps eventually deploying, conventional ballistic missiles, and possibly also hypersonic delivery vehicles, would present an entirely new type of threat. Capable of reaching China from outside its defensive envelope, such weapons would sidestep its increasingly extensive A2/AD network. Because they would largely circumvent existing defences, non-air-breathing systems would also present PLA planners with new, difficult and expensive technical and operational challenges. In contrast to the current, one-sided situation, in which it threatens its neighbours with missiles but is not threatened in return, China too would have to worry about a conventional ballistic-missile attack.

Reassurance

In addition to shaping the weapons programmes and crisis decision-making of potential enemies, ASB aims to influence the behaviour of Washington's friends. As the ASBO's May 2013 paper explains, 'continued US investments in the capabilities identified in the concept reassure our allies and partners, and demonstrate that the US will not retreat from, or submit to, potential aggressors who would otherwise try to defy the international community the right to international waters and airspace.'[49] By demonstrating that it has the means and the determination to fight, the US hopes to bolster the resolve of its partners, encouraging them to cooperate more closely and to make greater efforts on their own behalf.

While it is possible, on balance, that the adoption of ASB will have these effects, the actual responses of US allies are likely to be more varied. Uncertainty over what exactly ASB is, and what it implies for their own forces and strategy, has caused puzzlement and anxiety in some foreign capitals. If ASB is implemented in a way that reduces reliance on forward bases and forward-deployed forces, this could raise concerns that, no matter what it says, Washington is edging away from its commitments in Asia. Because it would be less susceptible to pre-emption, such a posture might seem ideal from a purely war-fighting perspective, but pulling forces back from the theatre would undercut Washington's efforts to reassure its allies. If it was seen as a signal that the US was decoupling from its allies, such a move could also end up weakening deterrence and increasing the risk of war.

None of the United States' friends are eager to be seen as signing up to policies that could lead to increased tensions with China. The offensive aspect of ASB – the fact that it would involve strikes against targets on the Chinese mainland, some of which would likely be launched from allied soil – is especially troubling in this regard. Warnings about the risk of nuclear escalation from ASB critics in the West, if not directly from Beijing, only heighten these anxieties. Fears of confrontation in allied capitals are offset by concerns over China's growing capabilities and increasing aggressiveness. These concerns are causing at least some US allies to cooperate more closely with Washington in balancing Chinese power, albeit to varying degrees. Because of its location and capabilities, Japan is the most important potential contributor to ASB; thanks to its already fraught relations with China, it is also clearly the most receptive and the most likely to be reassured by a more forward-leaning American posture. Of the remaining major US allies in East Asia, South Korea currently seems the least likely to see its interests served by any direct involvement with the new concept, while Australia falls somewhere in between.[50]

Implications

ASB identifies a set of operational tasks – disrupting the enemy's C4ISR, destroying its A2/AD systems and defeating its weapons after they have been launched – but does not specify how to carry them out. The manner in which the US military prepares to accomplish these three missions will go a long way towards shaping its budgets, research-and-development programmes and force posture. While many different combinations of weapons and tactics are conceivable, it may be helpful to distinguish between a linear and a discontinuous approach to ASB. The approaches are not mutually exclusive and, depending on the availability of resources and the evolution of the threat, could be implemented sequentially or simultaneously. In general, the first approach aims to offset the effects of China's build-up through the steady deployment of existing systems, while the second places greater emphasis on developing new and potentially game-changing weapons (see Table 1).

Linear approach

The linear variant of ASB would seek to implement the concept with comparatively small changes in existing plans and programmes. For purposes of disrupting the PLA's C4ISR

Table 1: **Alternative approaches to Air–Sea Battle**

	Disrupt	Defeat	Destroy
Linear	Cyber and electronic warfare B-2 Joint Air-to-Surface Standoff Missile (JASSM) Submarine-launched cruise missile (SLCM) Next-Generation Bomber (NGB)	Kinetic-kill weapons (Terminal High Altitude Area Defense, *Patriot* Advanced Capability-3, Standard Missile-3) Passive defences	F-35, F-22, B-2, B-1 NGB JASSM SLCM
Discontinuous*	Conventional submarine-launched ballistic missile (SLBM) Global Precision Strike	Directed-energy (DE) weapons	Conventional SLBM Hypersonic cruise missile Unmanned autonomous aerial vehicle

*A discontinuous approach would combine some mix of the same systems deployed under the linear variant of ASB as well as new types of weapons. For purposes of clarity, only the latter are listed here.

systems, cyber and EW attacks would be heavily relied upon. Critical nodes located close to China's coasts could be attacked with submarine-launched cruise missiles; stand-off air-to-surface missiles (including the Joint Air-to-Surface Standoff Missile), launched from aircraft hundreds of miles from their targets; and shorter-range weapons (including the Joint Direct Attack Munition and the Joint Standoff Weapon). The latter could be delivered by stealthy aircraft (presumably including F-35s and F-22s, as well as the longer-range B-2, perhaps supplemented eventually by a carrier-launched unmanned aerial vehicle), operating inside the envelope of the PLA's air-defence systems. Facilities located deep in the Chinese interior would have to be targeted by B-2 bombers, the only platform capable of delivering conventional weapons against them.[51]

The task of destroying China's land-based A2/AD weapons and platforms would be assigned to the same mixture of systems: precision-guided weapons and cruise missiles, of varying ranges, launched from manned stand-off and pene-trating aircraft, submarines and surface vessels. Because of the difficulty of acquiring reliable information on the location of mobile targets, and because existing platforms have only a very limited capacity to loiter over enemy territory, the bulk of this effort would have to be directed at fixed facilities. Chinese cruise and ballistic missiles that had been dispersed into the field would therefore be likely to survive, although their subsequent use could reveal new targets for a follow-on attack.

In order to defeat Chinese missiles after their launch, the US and its allies would rely on a mixture of active and passive defences. Current plans call for the deployment of a land-based, high-altitude ballistic-missile defence system (Terminal High Altitude Area Defense, or THAAD) to supplement existing shorter-range systems (such as the *Patriot* Advanced Capability-3, or PAC-3) around ports, airfields and command facilities, as well as an increase in the number of ship-based interceptors (such as the Standard Missile-3, or SM-3). These programmes could be expanded or accelerated at the margins, as could the so-called Pacific Airpower Resiliency Initiative, under which the air force is investing more in hardened hangars, runway repair kits, firefighting capabilities, camouflage and preparations for the emergency dispersal and concealment of aircraft.[52]

Discontinuous approach
Instead of relying heavily on existing programmes, under a discontinuous approach to ASB, the DoD would shift more resources towards developing novel means of performing the concept's three core missions. In order to ensure the prompt disruption of C4ISR systems, regardless of their location, the US might supplement cyber and EW attacks with strikes by conventionally armed ballistic missiles. While investments in passive defences would continue, resources would be reallocated away from the further expansion of existing kinetic-kill missile defences and towards the rapid development and deployment of DE weapons for the defence of both naval and land-based targets.[53] Fixed elements of China's A2/AD system

would still be engaged and destroyed with cruise missiles and gravity bombs. Assuming that they can be located, mobile missiles could be vulnerable to prompt strikes by very high-speed weapons, either conventional ballistic missiles, fired either from submarines or possibly at intercontinental range, or hypersonic cruise missiles launched from submarines or stand-off bombers. Alternatively, the US might accelerate its efforts to develop stealthy, long-endurance autonomous aerial vehicles capable of locating and destroying Chinese mobile missiles.

Because it would rely primarily on existing systems, the linear version of ASB would carry relatively little technological risk and could be implemented without delay. Although the extent to which various programmes would be funded remains to be determined, this appears to be the approach that the DoD is currently following. Sticking with some version of the Program of Record would also mean continuing to spend a sizeable portion of available resources on relatively small numbers of selected, very expensive platforms, including manned fighters and nuclear-powered attack submarines. In a period of tight budgets, less money would therefore be available for the development of new, and potentially more cost-effective, weapons.

Whatever its impact on defence budgets, the strategic risks associated with the linear approach could be substantial. If cyber and EW attacks are not as effective at disabling China's C4ISR network as is anticipated, allied defences fail to dramatically reduce the impact of a Chinese first strike and/or the People's Liberation Army Air Force (PLAAF) succeeds in developing defences against stealthy air-breathing weapons, the US could find itself incapable of achieving some of its key military objectives in the opening stage of a war. Pressing ahead with familiar systems and approaches also seems less likely to present China with difficult new problems. Creating such problems could help to bolster deterrence by heightening uncertainty or shift the dynamic of the long-term competition by forcing the PLA to embark on costly new programmes.

A discontinuous version of ASB would invert the advantages and disadvantages of the linear approach. If successful, new systems such as DE weapons and autonomous aerial vehicles could provide more cost-effective ways of achieving key objectives, greatly complicating the situation confronting PLA planners and shifting the ongoing military competition in directions more favourable to the US. There is always a danger, however, that cost overruns and unexpected technical challenges could soak up scarce resources, delaying the fielding of new capabilities, and perhaps leaving the US worse off, on balance, than if it had held to a more conservative course.

Notes

[1] Leon Panetta, 'Sustaining US Global Leadership: Priorities for 21st Century Defense', January 2012, p. 4, http://www.defense.gov/news/defense_strateg c_guidance.pdf. This document is intended to identify priorities and provide strategic guidance for the armed services and the DoD as a whole.

[2] ASBO, 'Air-Sea Battle: Service Collaboration to Address Anti-Access and Area Denial Challenges', Washington DC, May 2013, p. 1. Some observers claim that a 'Pacific Vision' war game conducted in October 2008 helped drive home the importance of addressing the problem. See Richard Halloran, 'PACAF's "Vision Thing"', Air Force Magazine, vol. 92, no. 1, January 2009, pp. 54–6. There were also reports of heightened tensions and concerns over possible Chinese military action against Taiwan prior to the March 2008 presidential election. Wu Ming-chieh, 'US feared cross-strait clash before 2008 election: Wikileaks', Want China Times, 9 September 2011, http://www.wantchinatimes.com/news-subclass-cnt.aspx?id=20110911000007&cid=1101.

[3] Office of the Secretary of Defense, Quadrennial Defense Review Report (Washington DC: DoD, February 2010), p. 32.

[4] DoD, Joint Operational Access Concept (JOAC) Version 1.0, 22 November 2011. A final, official version of this document was signed in January 2012. See http://www.defense.gov/pubs/pdfs/joac_jan%202012_signed.pdf.

5   DoD, 'Background Briefing on Air-Sea Battle by Defense Officials from the Pentagon', 9 November 2011, http://www.defense.gov/transcripts/transcript.aspx?transcriptid=4923. In the hierarchy of DoD concepts and planning documents, ASB is a more specific and focused application of the general approaches spelled out in the JOAC. The JOAC flows from 'Joint Force 2020' (also known as the 'Capstone Concept for Joint Operations' or CCJO), the chairman of the Joint Chiefs of Staff's overall vision for the development of the armed forces. That document is the military's response to the highest-level DoD Strategic Guidance (DSG), which comes directly from the defence secretary and the president.

6   Norton Schwartz, 'Remarks to the National Defense University Distinguished Lecture Program', 15 December 2010, p. 2, http://www.afoutreach.af.mil/shared/media/document/AFD-110414-062.pdf.

7   Norton Schwartz, 'Joint CSAF–CNO Discussion on the Air–Sea Battle Concept', Brookings Institution, Washington DC, 16 May 2012.

8   Norton Schwartz and Jonathan Greenert, 'Air-Sea Battle: Promoting Stability in an Era of Uncertainty', American Interest, 20 February 2012, http://www.the-american-interest.com/article.cfm?piece=1212.

9   ASBO, 'Air-Sea Battle', p. 3.

10 DoD, Joint Operational Access Concept (JOAC) version 1.0, p. 5.

11 Panetta, 'Sustaining US Global Leadership', p. 4.

12 DoD, Joint Operational Access Concept (JOAC) version 1.0, pp. ii, 16.

13 Ibid., p. 17.

14 ASBO, 'Air-Sea Battle', pp. 3–4.

15 Ibid., p. 4.

16 Ibid., p. 5.

17 Ibid., pp. 6–7.

18 Ibid., p. 7. In their 2012 article, Greenert and Schwartz describe the three lines of effort in slightly greater detail: 'offensive operations to deceive and deny adversary battle networks, particularly intelligence, surveillance and reconnaissance (ISR) and command and control (C2) systems ... offensive operations to neutralize adversary weapon delivery platforms such as ships, submarines, aircraft, and missile launchers ... [and] defensive operations to protect joint forces and their enablers from weapons launched by an adversary.' Schwartz and Greenert, 'Air-Sea Battle'.

19 Jonathan Greenert and Mark Welsh, 'Breaking the Kill Chain', Foreign Policy, 16 May 2013, http://www.foreignpolicy.com/articles/2013/05/16/breaking_the_kill_chain_air_sea_battle.

20 In a brief discussion of states that might employ A2/AD capabilities, Greenert and Welsh mention Iran, North Korea and Syria but not China. Regarding the difficulties of planning for a possible conflict against a threat that cannot be named, see J. Randy Forbes, 'China. There, I Said It', PacNet, no. 34, 5 June 2012, http://csis.org/files/publication/Pac1234.pdf.

21 Jan van Tol et al., AirSea Battle: A Point-of-Departure Operational Concept (Washington DC: Center for Strategic and Budgetary Assessments, 2010), p. 53.

22 Ibid., p. 57.

23 *Ibid.*, p. 58.

24 *Ibid.*, pp. 64–6.

25 See Sydney J. Freedberg, Jr, 'Army Targets AirSea Battle; Hungers for Pacific Role', *Breaking Defense*, 13 December 2011, http://defense. aol.com/2011/12/13/army-targets-airsea-battle-hungers-for-pacific-role/; Greg Fontenot and Kevin Benson, 'Way of War or the Latest "Fad"? A Critique of AirSea Battle', *Infinity Journal*, vol. 2, no. 4, https/www.infinityjournal. com/article/82/Way_of_War_ or_the_Latest_Fad_A_critique_ of_AirSea_Battle/; and Douglas Macgregor and Young J. Kim, 'Air-Sea Battle: Something's Missing', *Armed Forces Journal*, April 2012, http://www.armedforces journal. com/2012/04/9772607/. The role of ground forces in countering A2/AD threats in various regions, including the Pacific, is described in US Army Capabilities Integration Center and US Marine Corps Combat Development Command, 'Gaining and Maintaining Access: An Army-Marine Corps Concept', March 2012, http://www. defenseinnovationmarketplace.mil/ resources/Army%20Marine%20 Corp%20Gaining% 20and%20 Maintaining%20Access.pdf.

26 J. Noel Williams, 'Air-Sea Battle: An Operational Concept Looking for a Strategy', *Armed Forces Journal*, September 2011, http:// www.armedforcesjournal. com/2011/09/7558138/.

27 T.X. Hammes, 'AirSea Battle Isn't about China', *National Interest*, 19 October 2012, http:// nationalinterest.org/commentary/ airsea-battle-isnt-about-china-7627.

28 ASBO, 'Air-Sea Battle', p. 1.

29 DoD, *Joint Operational Access Concept (JOAC) version 1.0*, pp. 3–4. These comments apply fully to ASB even though it is technically only one possible variant of the overarching JOAC.

30 Nathan K. Finney, 'Air-Sea Battle as a Military Contribution to Strategy Development', *Infinity Journal*, vol. 2, no. 4, Autumn 2012, p. 9, https://www.infinityjournal. com/article/79/AirSea_Battle_ as_a_Military_Contribution_to_ Strategy_D evelopment/.

31 DoD, 'Background Briefing on Air-Sea Battle by Defense Officials from the Pentagon'.

32 For a discussion of the possible benefits of missile-defence systems that rely on directed energy, see the section on long-term competition, p. 91.

33 Van Tol, *AirSea Battle*, p. 65.

34 Chinese analysts have discussed 'the application of nuclear weapons used to carry out active and passive deterrence' for a variety of purposes, including preventing 'the enemy from carrying out a conventional strike against our nuclear facilities' or causing 'huge, unrecoverable losses to our major, strategic facilities through high-powered air raids against us'. Yu Jixun (ed.), *The Science of Second Artillery Campaigns* (Beijing: PLA Press, 2004), p. 223.

35 See Elbridge Colby, 'Don't Sweat AirSea Battle', *National Interest*, 31 July 2013, http:// nationalinterest.org/commentary/ dont-sweat-airsea-battle-8804.

36 The US presently has over 4,000 strategic nuclear warheads, while China is believed to have around

30. By 2020, according to some estimates, the US arsenal could shrink to around 1,500 while the Chinese force grows into the hundreds. Regarding US forces, see Hans M. Kristensen, *Trimming Nuclear Excess: Options for Further Reductions of US and Russian Nuclear Forces* (Washington DC: Federation of American Scientists, 2012). Estimates of the size of the Chinese force, at that time, range from around 100 to over 600 warheads with long-range delivery systems. See Aaron L. Friedberg, *A Contest for Supremacy: China, America and the Struggle for Mastery in Asia* (New York: W.W. Norton & Company, 2011), p. 227.

[37] As Elbridge Colby points out, 'even in the event of a major war, both the United States and China would have the weightiest possible reasons not to escalate to a nuclear exchange'. Colby, 'Don't Sweat AirSea Battle'. Of course, in the event of war, Beijing might not behave rationally. For a discussion of how misperceptions and domestic political pressures could push China's leaders towards nuclear escalation, despite the evident dangers, see Joshua Rovner, 'Three Paths to Nuclear Escalation with China', *National Interest*, 19 July 2012, http://nationalinterest. org/blog/the-skeptics/three-paths-nuclear-escalation-china-7216.

[38] *Ibid.* See also Raoul Heinrichs, 'America's Dangerous Battle Plan', *Diplomat*, 17 August 2011, http:// thediplomat.com/2011/08/17/ america's-dangerous-battle-plan. To the contrary, Christopher Ford argues that even successful ASB attacks on 'Chinese regional ISR capabilities, long-range strike systems, and associated C2' are unlikely to provoke nuclear escalation because these are not 'core strategic assets of the Chinese regime'. Christopher Ford, '"Air/ Sea Battle", Escalation, and US Strategy in the Pacific', PJ Media, 6 January 2013, http://pjmedia.com/ blog/airsea-battle-escalation-and-u-s-strategy-in-the -Pacific.

[39] See Steven Pifer, 'Nuclear Arms: Obama Visits Berlin – and Returns to Prague', *Brookings Up Front*, 19 June 2013, http://www.brookings.edu/ blogs/up-front/posts/2013/06/19-nuclear-arms-reductions-obama-berlin-pifer.

[40] Thomas Schelling, *The Strategy of Conflict* (Cambridge, MA: Harvard University Press, 1990).

[41] Conventional counter-attacks are not the only means for achieving this end. Others, including economic blockades, are discussed in Chapter Four.

[42] See the discussion of this issue in Avery Goldstein, 'First Things First: The Pressing Danger of Crisis Instability in US-China Relations', *International Security*, vol. 37, no. 4, Spring 2013, pp. 66–8.

[43] By one estimate, super-hardened shelters capable of defeating ballistic and cruise missiles with penetrating warheads would cost on the order of US$700 million but could protect over US$10 billion of US Air Force assets. John Stillton, 'Fighting Under Missile Attack', *Air Force Magazine*, August 2009, p. 37.

[44] Mark Gunzinger and Chris Dougherty, *Changing the Game: The Promise of Directed Energy Weapons* (Washington DC: Center

for Strategic and Budgetary Assessments, 2012), p. ix.

[45] According to one recent study, of the US$267.9bn to be spent between FY2010 and FY2016 on what is described as 'Air-Sea Battle related procurement and RDT&E', US$82bn, or roughly 30%, will fund the F-35. Research and Markets, 'Air-Sea Battle Concepts, Key Programs and Forecast', G2 Solutions, January 2012, http://www.researchandmarkets.com/reports/2064421/.

[46] Adding the so-called Virginia Payload Modules (VPMs) to *Virginia*-class nuclear-attack submarines could increase their capacity for land-attack cruise missiles by 76%, from a maximum of 37 to a total of 65. (In practice, some of the available launch tubes would be used for other purposes, including launching torpedoes and deploying special-operations forces.) This would help offset the dramatic drop in available weapons that will otherwise accompany the retirement of older *Ohio*-class boats, which have been converted into cruise-missile carriers. However, the VPMs are expensive (potentially adding around 20% to the over-US$2bn price tag for each submarine, and possibly necessitating a cut in the total number of boats procured), the *Tomahawk* cruise missiles they carry have a range of roughly 1,000 miles, and the total number of missiles available would be in the order of 1,000. This would allow ample coverage of targets relatively close to China's coasts but not those further inland. Ronald O'Rourke, *Navy Virginia (SSN-774)*

Class Attack Submarine Procurement: Background and Issues for Congress (Washington DC: Congressional Research Service, 2012), pp. 6–7. In part because paying for the VPM will eat into the navy's shipbuilding budget, the programme's future is now in doubt. See Elaine M. Grossman, 'Pentagon, Lawmakers Deal Blows to Navy Fast-Strike Missile Effort', Global Security Newswire, 31 July 2013, http://www.nti.org/gsn/article/pentagon-lawmakers-deal-blows-navy-fast-strike-missile-effort/.

[47] The DoD is committed to developing a new bomber, but this is not expected to reach initial operational capability until 'some time during the 2020s'. Kris Osborn, 'Next Generation Bomber Survives Budget Tightening', Defense Tech, 22 April 2013, http://defensetech.org/2013/04/22/next-generation-bomber-survives-budget-tightening/. In early 2012, Secretary of Defense Panetta announced a programme to develop a sea-launched conventional ballistic missile. See DoD, 'Defense Budget Priorities and Choices', January 2012, p. 5, http://www.defense.gov/news/Defense_Budget_Priorities.pdf. Funding for this programme is also in doubt. Grossman, 'Pentagon, Lawmakers Deal Blows to Navy Fast-Strike Missile Effort'. Deploying a land-based intermediate-range ballistic missile would require the abrogation or renegotiation of the Intermediate-Range Nuclear Forces Treaty with Russia. For a discussion of the options for prompt global strike, see Amy F. Woolf, *Conventional Prompt*

Global Strike and Long-Range Ballistic Missiles: Background and Issues (Washington DC: Congressional Research Service, 2013).

48 One way of enhancing this threat that could impose disproportionate costs would be to demonstrate a capacity to attack Chinese targets from multiple directions, and not only from the east. This could be done both with long-range cruise missiles and manned penetrating bombers.

49 ASBO, 'Air-Sea Battle', p. i.

50 Australian responses to ASB are discussed in Benjamin Schreer, *Planning the Unthinkable War: 'AirSea Battle' and Its Implications for Australia* (Canberra: Australian Strategic Policy Institute, 2013). On possible Japanese roles in implementing ASB, see Sugio Takahashi, 'Counter A2/AD in Japan-U.S. Defense Cooperation: Toward "Allied Air-Sea Battle"', Project 2049 Institute, Washington DC, http://project2049.net/documents/counter_a2ad_defense_cooperation_takahashi.pdf. For a sample of South Korean views, see 'Korea-US alliance faces next crucial shift', *Korea Herald*, 21 August 2013, http://www.koreaherald.com/view.php?ud=20130821000752.

51 Greenert and Welsh appear to acknowledge (but discount) the difficulty of launching kinetic strikes on remote nodes in China's command-and-control network with currently programmed systems when they write: 'strikes against installations deep inland are not necessarily required in Air-Sea Battle because adversary C4ISR may be vulnerable to disruption.' Greenert and Welsh, 'Breaking the Kill Chain'.

52 John A. Tirpak, 'Fighting for Access', *Air Force Magazine*, July 2013, p. 25.

53 According to a recent report by the Congressional Research Service, 'Department of Defense (DOD) development work on high-energy military lasers, which has been underway for decades, has reached the point where lasers capable of countering certain surface and air targets at ranges of about a mile could be made ready for installation on Navy surface ships over the next few years. More powerful shipboard lasers, which could become ready for installation in subsequent years, could provide Navy surface ships with an ability to counter a wider range of surface and air targets at ranges of up to about 10 miles. These more powerful lasers might, among other things, provide Navy surface ships with a terminal-defense capability against certain ballistic missiles, including China's new anti-ship ballistic missile (ASBM).' Despite their potential, however, 'the Navy currently does not have a program of record for procuring a production version of a shipboard laser, or a roadmap that calls for installing lasers on specific surface ships by specific dates.' Ronald O'Rourke, *Navy Shipboard Lasers for Surface, Air, and Missile Defense: Background and Issues for Congress* (Washington DC: Congressional Research Service, 2013), p. 1.

CHAPTER FOUR

Indirect alternatives

Critics of Air–Sea Battle (ASB) have advanced alternative
military strategies that they believe could compel Beijing to
terminate hostilities, on terms acceptable to the United States
and its allies, at lower cost and with less risk of nuclear escalation. All of these proposals seek to avoid direct attacks on
Chinese territory while using air and naval operations to exert
economic and military pressure. Although some analysts have
suggested that the two lines of operation should be combined
for maximum effect, most draw a distinction between a
blockade that would begin just off China's coast and one that
would be put in place along the perimeter of the so-called 'first
island chain'.[1]

Distant blockade

As its label suggests, as part of a distant blockade, US and allied
air and naval forces (possibly backstopped by land-based anti-
ship cruise missiles) would seek to prevent shipping bound
for China from passing through a few narrow choke points
far removed from its own territory.[2] The simplest variant of
this plan would focus on stopping, seizing or diverting large

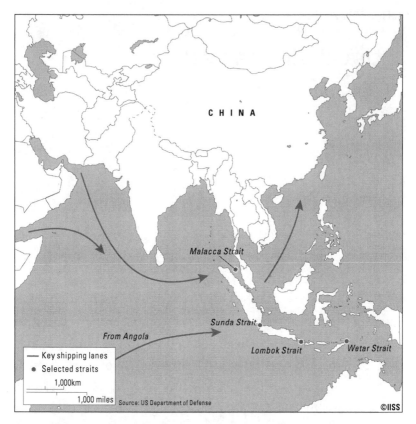

Map 3: **China's energy-import transit routes and possible choke points**

oil tankers as they approached the Malacca Strait at the south-ernmost opening of the South China Sea, or the Lombok and Sunda straits that pass between the islands of the Indonesian archipelago further to the east.

China already imports over half of the oil it consumes, a proportion that could grow to 80% by 2030.[3] The vast majority of these imports come from the Middle East and Africa (78% in 2011),[4] and, at present, most transit through the Malacca Strait (80% in 2012).[5] As China's import dependence grows, closing a handful of vital choke points would quickly and dramatically constrict its access to seaborne oil, which could have a far-reaching and potentially devastating impact on its economy, social stability and war-making capacity. Even if the effects were not immediate, a sustained blockade would impose rising costs on Beijing, perhaps forcing it to eventually sue for peace.

Advocates draw a comparison to the actions of the British Royal Navy during the First World War. Rather than sallying forth to battle, the British used their superior offshore geographical position to bottle up Germany's fleet, depriving its continental rival of access to overseas trade and helping to eventually defeat it. Similarly, instead of sailing directly into the enemy's anti-access/area-denial (A2/AD) capabilities, the US and its allies might be able to stand off beyond the range of China's forces and subject it to gradual economic strangulation.

Although it would impose painful pressure on the enemy, a distant energy blockade would not require direct attacks on Chinese soil and would have the added benefit of being readily reversible. For these reasons, it might cost fewer Chinese lives, do less lasting damage and be less likely to provoke escalation than the wide-ranging conventional strikes envisioned under ASB. In the words of Douglas Peifer, a distant blockade is 'a viable, lower cost strategy that capitalizes on America's strengths and China's weaknesses'.[6]

Assessment
War fighting
Even critics of the concept acknowledge that, at least for some time to come, it will be very difficult for China to mount a direct military challenge to a distant blockade. The key choke points are beyond the reach of current land-based ballistic missiles and either outside or at the very limit of the effective range of most Chinese aircraft, submarines and surface vessels. Any forces sent to disrupt or break a blockade would likely be detected, tracked and destroyed long before they could reach their intended targets.[7]

The primary obstacles to an effective blockade are logistical, diplomatic and possibly legal, rather than purely military. In their survey of the problems involved, Gabriel Collins and William Murray note that US and allied forces would have to stop and board hundreds of oil tankers to examine their bills of lading and determine their final destination.[8] Vessels obviously headed for China would be diverted to other ports or marshalling areas; those that refused to cooperate would be seized and manned by suitably trained 'prize crews'. Complicating matters considerably is the fact that few of the ships involved would actually be flying the Chinese flag and some might carry false or misleading papers. Once through a choke point, some tankers could simply change course or deliver their cargo to third-party ports, where it would be reloaded onto vessels bound for China. Efforts to prevent this could lead to serious tensions with neutral and perhaps even friendly governments, which, unless they shared US goals, would likely object to interference with their shipping.[9]

Collins and Murray estimate that a distant blockade would require a minimum of 16 surface vessels, four replenishment ships and an unspecified number of additional units to relieve the initial force, as well as other ships, submarines and aircraft to provide protection against attempted attacks by Chinese forces.[10] Mobilising such a flotilla would hardly be beyond the capacities of the US Navy, even one diminished in size by impending budget cuts. The burden on the fleet could be lessened further if some of the interceptions and boardings were done by comparatively lightly armed vessels (possibly including forward-deployed coastguard cutters), perhaps supported by allied navies.

Assuming that it could be successfully imposed, whether a blockade would have decisive effects on China's willingness and ability to wage war and, if so, how long these would take to make themselves felt depends on an array of economic, military and societal factors. These include: the size of China's strategic petroleum reserve; the ability of the government to reduce civilian demand; the rates at which fuel and other petroleum products were being consumed to conduct military operations; the capacity and security of overland oil and gas pipelines that bypassed maritime choke points; whether the US employed non-kinetic or covert means to shut down parts of China's energy infrastructure; and the population's response to a potentially protracted period of economic hardship.

Some of these factors are easier to predict and model than others. A 2006 study estimated that a blockade could cut China's total oil consumption by one-third, '[wiping] out over 8 percent of China's annual GDP growth' during the course of a year and bringing the economy 'to a standstill'. The authors acknowledge, however, that these estimates may well be inaccurate, and probably overstate the immediate impact of an embargo, in part because 'oil price and energy consumption elasticity coefficients might change in unexpected ways if the Chinese economy shifted to a war footing.'[11] Applying more recent data to the same model led Sean Mirski to conclude that a total cut-off of oil imports would cause a 12.5% contraction in China's GDP.[12]

Whatever its eventual impact, a distant blockade would take time to bite. In the interim, unless it was simultaneously conducting other offensive operations, the US would have done nothing to weaken Chinese forces or dislodge them from any positions they had acquired during initial attacks. The British blockade of Germany during the First World War, and the United States' maritime campaign against Japanese shipping during the Second World War, contributed to the eventual outcome of those conflicts, but only after several years and in combination with terrible damage inflicted on land and in the air.

A major selling point of a distant blockade is the claim that it is less likely to lead to escalation than a strategy that calls for airstrikes on Chinese territory. While it might not initially involve sinking ships or taking lives, the imposition of a blockade would nevertheless be an act of war, and it would be imprudent to expect that it would not provoke some kind of forceful response from China. As to the possibility of escalation once a war was clearly under way, it may be true that, in the opening phases of a conflict, the interdiction of shipping would appear less threatening to regime survival, and hence less likely to provoke an extreme response than attacks on command-and-control networks. If it worked, however, an energy blockade would put China's leaders in an increasingly desperate position; indeed, that would be precisely its purpose. While it is possible that mounting economic pressure and fear of internal unrest would cause Beijing to back down and make peace, an aggressive, escalatory reaction is equally plausible.

Deterrence

There is ample evidence to suggest that Chinese planners and strategists are worried about the possibility of a distant blockade. Former president Hu Jintao's reported reference to the 'Malacca Dilemma' at a Chinese Communist Party (CCP) economic work conference in 2003 was followed by a stream of articles and statements about the nature and extent of the problem, and possible solutions to it.[13] While these contain a range of opinions, one recent survey concludes that 'a wide variety of influential Chinese experts, including scholars, policy analysts, and members of the military, believe that the United States can sever China's seaborne energy supplies at will and in a crisis might well choose to do so.'[14] Some of those highlighting the potential danger are no doubt motivated by parochial concerns, including the desire to win infrastructure construction contracts or gain support for an expanded PLAN budget. Nonetheless, the sheer volume and diverse sources of commentary on this topic suggest that it is a serious concern for the top leadership. This impression is reinforced by the fact that, in the ten years since Hu's speech, Chinese companies have contemplated, initiated and expanded port and pipeline projects whose primary rationale appears to be their ability to bypass the Malacca Strait.[15]

Whether the threat of a distant blockade would deter Beijing from using force will depend on what is at stake in a particular crisis, whether the leadership believes that Washington would be willing and able to impose and maintain a blockade, and how China assesses the likely economic, military and societal effects in both the short and longer term. China's leaders have been sufficiently worried about the impact of a blockade to make significant investments to hedge against it. In a protracted conflict, the loss of access to seaborne energy imports might well have a decisive effect; but this does not necessarily mean that, on the brink of war, the threat of a distant blockade alone would prove to be an adequate deterrent.

Chinese planners may assess that their investments in pipelines (perhaps combined with the development of energy resources closer to home in the East and South China seas) have solved, or at least mitigated, the problem.[16] Even if they believe that the US would impose a blockade, they may be confident that they can erode its effectiveness through a combination of diplomatic pressure on other governments, an information campaign highlighting the hardships imposed on the Chinese people, and appeals to international law and multilateral institutions. Finally, political leaders may choose to accept military commanders' promises that they can deliver a swift and decisive victory, imposing a fait accompli before the Americans can bring the full weight of their power to bear.

Long-term competition

The threat to China's energy supplies posed by American naval power appears to be existential in two senses of the word; it is an inescapable feature of the current strategic environment and, if exercised, could bring about the defeat and collapse of the CCP regime. China will, therefore, have to exert great effort if it wants to escape, or even substantially mitigate, its current vulnerability. This could have important implications for its long-term competition with the US.

Although the motivations and funding of the enterprises involved are not always transparent, it seems that many of the pipeline projects that have sprung up around China's interior periphery in the past decade have a strategic, as well as economic, rationale. Similarly, in addition to their commercial value, the ports and other facilities that Chinese companies are building around the rim of the Indian Ocean, including in Bangladesh, Pakistan, Sri Lanka and the Maldives, may be part of a long-term effort to enhance China's ability to protect the sea lanes that extend from the Malacca Strait to the Straits of Hormuz, at the mouth of the Persian Gulf. The People's Liberation Army Navy's (PLAN) participation in anti-piracy operations near the Horn of Africa, its role in evacuating Chinese nationals from Libya, as well as recent comments by an outspoken admiral that China should seek access to overseas bases, all point in a similar direction.[17]

Beijing's anxieties about energy security are thus already causing it to expend resources that might otherwise be directed elsewhere. Most of this money is going towards civilian projects and the impact on defence programmes has so far been small. To have a chance of securing its vital sea lines, China will ultimately have to spend far more, with potentially far-reaching effects on the size and structure of its military budget. Barring a revolutionary change in the location of exploitable energy deposits and transportation routes, the only other choice will be to learn to live with perpetual vulnerability, a distinctly unappealing prospect for an aspiring global power.[18] In the words of one Chinese analyst:

> A big country that builds its prosperity on foreign trade cannot put the safety of its ocean fleet in the hands of other countries. Doing so would be the equivalent of placing its throat under another's dagger and marking its blood vessels in red ink.[19]

For the moment, China's naval development, along with much of its build-up of land-based air and missile forces, is directed primarily at denying an enemy access to its near seas (the waters between China's coast and the first island chain). In the long run, however, if it is to free itself from the threat of a distant blockade, the People's Republic of China (PRC) will have to develop new and different capabilities, most likely including big-deck aircraft carriers, nuclear submarines, surface combatants able to defend themselves against air and missile attacks, and a small armada of under-way refuelling and replenishment ships, all capable of circumnavigating the globe. As is true of the US Navy, the PLAN's ability to sustain substantial forces on station, at great distances from home, will depend on access to local bases and facilities for repair, rearming and refuelling.[20]

All of this will take time and cost a great deal of money. As China's growth rates begin to decline over coming decades, the pursuit of greatly expanded naval capabilities will likely add to the military's share of GDP and intensify inter-service disputes over missions and budget allocations. Whether the US and its allies should fear or welcome China's attempts to develop a true 'blue water' navy (one that can operate in open oceans worldwide) is open to debate. If it succeeds, Beijing will eventually be able to exert influence and defend its interests on a truly global scale, while challenging those of the US. In the long interval before it can do any of this effectively, however, China will expend scarce resources on systems that will likely pose a less immediate threat than those it is deploying closer to home, and may in fact be quite vulnerable to existing American and allied weapons. It will also try to develop the capacity to perform complex tasks, such as launching air-strikes from carriers and conducting open-ocean, anti-submarine warfare (ASW) operations, which have taken other countries generations to perfect.

Simply by virtue of its size, capabilities and patterns of deployment, the US Navy poses a threat to China's energy supply lines. Even if it wanted to, Washington could not convince Beijing that it would never, under any circumstances, try to take advantage of this potential vulnerability. While doing so would risk feeding fears of encirclement and could provoke heightened belligerence, because of its likely impact on China's long-term military development, American planners may nevertheless seek ways to quietly play on existing anxieties about energy security. These might include conducting war games prominently featuring interdiction scenarios, joint training exercises with allies, and the forward deployment of ships, aircraft and possibly missiles that could be used to impose a blockade.

Reassurance

Will Washington's Asian allies be reassured by a strategy that places reliance on the threat of a distant blockade to deter or defeat Chinese aggression? Because it could be cloaked in talk of enhancing maritime security and would not require major shifts in force posture or overt participation in planning for attacks on Chinese territory, such an approach might be appealing to nervous policymakers in some foreign capitals. However, those on the front lines, either on or inside the periphery of the first island chain, would likely find it less attractive. Observers in Japan, Taiwan and the Philippines, for example, have cause for concern that the imposition of a distant blockade, in response to Chinese aggression, will be insufficient to defend their interests and protect their territory. If China conquered Taiwan, or seized disputed islands in the East China Sea and dug in to defend them, closing the Malacca Strait would do little to force Beijing to disgorge its gains in the short run.[21]

Standing off at a distance rather than challenging China in its own backyard may make sense in purely military terms. However, if the US appears willing to cede control of China's near seas, its behaviour could be interpreted by others as a sign of weakness and perhaps of a lack of commitment to the long-term security of its friends. If China can force it to withdraw from the Western Pacific, the United States' days as the preponderant regional power are surely numbered, and China's emergence in that role would be at hand. More concretely, unless the US Navy is prepared to do more than merely take up defensive positions along the perimeter, it will leave China free to harass neutral and allied shipping plying the waters within the first island chain.

Implications
A distant-blockade strategy could be implemented with forces that, for the most part, already exist. Even if the estimate by Collins and Murray that only 16 ships at a time would be required to close off the main passages into the South China Sea is low, it is not very far off. What is more, the types of weapons necessary to impose a distant blockade would be neither the

most expensive nor the most capable in the current inventory. Because they would operate outside the range of China's A2/AD systems, the US and its allies could rely on ships and aircraft that are comparatively lightly armed and defended. As Mirski notes, 'the US Navy's recent acquisitions, however, troubled their developmental histories, would be ideal for the purposes of a blockade.' Even the 'much-maligned' Littoral Combat Ship (LCS) could be useful in this regard.[22] Whatever the thinking behind it, the decision to base several of these vessels in Singapore, at the mouth of the Malacca Strait, cannot help but be seen in Beijing as a reminder that the US is in a position to threaten China's energy supply.

Reliance on a distant-blockade strategy would likely mean increased budget shares for lightly armed and armoured surface vessels; relatively inexpensive anti-ship cruise missiles that could be fired from air, land or sea; maritime patrol aircraft; devices for tagging and tracking commercial ships; training for the interdiction and seizure of ships at sea; and command, control, communications, computers, intelligence, surveillance and reconnaissance (C4ISR) systems that would enable greater domain awareness and a more rapid exchange of information with allied forces. Nonetheless, of the concepts considered here, a distant blockade would have the least dramatic implications for force posture and defence budgets.

Maritime denial

The third potential response to China's growing A2/AD capabilities would also be indirect, in the sense that it would seek to avoid a direct attack on the Chinese mainland, but would call for operations that are considerably more aggressive than those of a distant blockade. Several variants of this idea have been advanced, along with different labels, including 'war-at-sea', 'offshore control' and 'mutually denied battlespace'. Perhaps most apt is the term 'maritime denial', suggested by Raoul Heinrichs of the Australian National University.[23]

A maritime-denial strategy would begin where the distant blockade left off. In addition to regulating the flow of oil tankers through a handful of remote choke points, US and allied forces would go on the offensive, sinking Chinese naval vessels and commercial shipping throughout the near seas. Small, fast coastal combatants armed with anti-ship cruise missiles, as well as missiles launched from shore batteries along the first island chain, could help to seal off some of the main approaches to China's coastal waters.[24] Within the inner seas, the bulk of the effort would be assigned to submarines and other undersea-warfare assets, possibly including sophisticated mines and unmanned underwater vehicles (UUVs). Proceeding in this way would effectively duck most of China's A2/AD network, which is aimed at aircraft and surface vessels, and move the fight into a domain in which the US and its allies retain significant advantages.

The goal of a maritime-denial campaign would be to create what Jeffrey Kline and Wayne Hughes have described as 'a maritime no-man's-land within the first island chain'.[25] In addition to being deprived of energy from the Persian Gulf, the PRC would be cut off from access to offshore supplies of oil and natural gas, including Russian seaborne deliveries. Indeed, it would lose the ability to use the sea for any purpose, such as coastal transport and the shipment of goods to overseas markets. Given that imports and exports account for over 50% of China's GDP[26] and that 85% of its international trade moves by sea, the impact on the nation's economy would be larger and more immediate than that of a distant energy blockade.[27]

Along with its economic effects, maritime denial would disrupt China's efforts to project military power. People's

Liberation Army (PLA) forces that had landed on Taiwan or seized disputed islands could find themselves cut off from seaborne supplies and reinforcements. If, in addition to attacking Chinese surface vessels, allied forces waged a successful campaign against enemy submarines, it might be possible to open at least some portions of the near seas to friendly commercial traffic. An aggressive ASW campaign, combined with the emplacement of anti-ship cruise missiles and undersea monitoring equipment on small islands in the Ryukyus, in parts of the Philippines archipelago and along the coast of South Korea, would also make it very difficult for PLAN surface ships or submarines to break out of the first island chain, into the wider waters of the Western Pacific.[28] Weakening Chinese forces and constricting the operational scope of those that survive would increase the odds of safe passage for friendly shipping to Japan and South Korea, enabling them to keep their economies running even as China's ground to a halt.

Assessment
War fighting
A maritime-denial strategy must be assessed by the same measures as a distant blockade: firstly, could US forces (perhaps alongside those of allies) succeed in carrying out their assigned missions? Secondly, if they did, what would be the impact on the conduct of the war? And thirdly, what are the chances that the execution of such a strategy would lead to nuclear escalation?

The first question can be subdivided into two parts: could US and allied forces deny China's surface ships the use of its near seas? And could they effectively clear those waters of Chinese submarines? The PLAN would face several substantial obstacles in trying to defend its combatants and commercial vessels from undersea attack. Because the ocean floor produces numerous false returns that can overload active sonar systems and conceal the presence of submarines, the shallow waters along China's coast are better suited to 'hiders' than to 'finders'. Heightening the challenge would be the fact that the PLAN has no real experience in conducting ASW operations and, until recently, invested very little in acquiring the requisite capabilities.[29]

For the moment, at least, American submarines could operate with relative impunity within the near seas. The major factors limiting their ability to disrupt shipping and sink naval vessels would be the logistical and communications difficulties caused by a presumed Chinese first strike, as well as the number of available submarines. Assuming that the US could compensate for the loss of some forward facilities by using expedient bases dispersed across the Western Pacific, at-sea replenishment and perhaps high-frequency radio to take the place of damaged satellites and ground stations, the availability of submarines would be decisive.

The US Navy currently has 55 nuclear-powered attack submarines, carrying torpedoes and anti-ship and cruise missiles, but that number could fall to 43 by the end of the coming decade.[30] Not all of these boats will be available for use in the Western Pacific; some are also slated to be modified so that they can carry more land-attack cruise missiles and fewer anti-ship weapons. For those that remain, the highest priorities in the opening phases of a war with China would be locating and sinking enemy submarines, as opposed to attacking surface vessels.

If they chose to take part, US allies could add considerable weight to an undersea campaign. Japan has 16 attack submarines, a force that will grow to at least 22 in the next few years.[31] South Korea currently has 12, with plans to build six more.[32] Australia presently has six, but plans to replace them over the next 15 years with 12 new ones, whose longer range would make it possible for them to participate in maritime-denial operations.[33] Depending on their location, allied forces might also be able to strike targets using air-, sea- and land-launched, long-range anti-ship cruise missiles, fired from the edges of China's A2/AD envelope.

The US and its allies may be able to deny Chinese surface vessels the use of the near seas, but this does not necessarily mean that they could guarantee such freedom for their own ships. As long as they are immune to attack, the land-based portions of China's A2/AD network will continue to function and enemy aircraft and surface vessels that come within its range will remain vulnerable, including those that might be used to conduct ASW operations. The same physical factors that complicate China's efforts to locate American and allied submarines would also provide a measure of protection for its own boats. As the PLAN deploys more, newer and quieter diesel submarines, the challenge will grow even greater. For these reasons, Owen Cote concludes that neither the US nor the PRC will have 'a robust ASW capability in China's coastal waters', which will therefore 'constitute a zone of "contested command" in which neither side can assure its use of the sea surface for either commercial or military purposes'.[34]

Hughes argues, similarly, that the immediate aim of maritime-denial operations should be to 'create a region where – at the outset of hostilities – *neither side* can operate safely on the surface', but he clearly regards this as a transitional phase.[35] Although he does not describe in detail how this could be done (particularly without attacking targets on the Chinese mainland), Hughes suggests elsewhere that US and allied forces should seek to eventually track and sink all Chinese attack submarines while protecting 'routes for innocent, friendly traffic into East Asian states'.[36]

Proponents claim that a maritime-denial strategy would subject China to immediate and dramatic pressure, without at the same time creating unacceptable risks of rapid escalation. As with a more limited blockade targeted only at energy supplies, the effects of a complete loss of access to the sea for China are, at this point, a matter of conjecture and assertion. It would certainly be dangerous to assume that maritime denial is a 'winning weapon', capable of bringing Beijing quickly to its knees. The regime would undoubtedly find ways to cope with shortages and work around obstacles while it put the nation on a war footing. Nonetheless, in light of the extent of China's growing reliance on imports of raw materials and food, as well as energy, and the degree to which its prosperity is dependent on exports, it seems likely that the dislocations would be severe and would grow worse with the passage of time.

In terms of its escalatory risk, maritime denial probably falls somewhere in between ASB and a distant blockade. In comparison to the latter, it involves early and violent action against Chinese personnel and property, even if these are not located on Chinese soil. However, the sinking of ships at sea, and even the mining of harbours, would not appear as immediately threatening to regime survival as attacks on missiles and command-and-control sites, which might be the start of a disarming first strike. That said, the assertion that such an approach is 'inherently de-escalating' seems overly sanguine.[37] Having taken their best shot at defeating the US with a quick knock-out blow, China's leaders would find themselves facing the prospect of a prolonged and debilitating struggle. While a negotiated settlement might seem the most prudent course, emotions would be running high, political careers (and perhaps regime survival) would be at stake and the leadership would face intense pressure from some quarters to redouble its efforts in pursuit of final victory.

Deterrence

Chinese strategists and policymakers often speak in general terms about threats from the sea and the importance of defending the nation's maritime approaches.[38] Michael Pillsbury reports that, in addition to their specific concerns about energy and the 'Malacca dilemma', Chinese planners worry about the imposition of a general blockade along the first island chain and the possible loss of access to resources within their own maritime boundaries. However, they do not appear to make a clear distinction between these dangers.[39] Assessing the relative deterrent efficacy of the threat of maritime denial, as compared to a distant blockade or ASB, is a matter of speculation. Which of these possibilities seems more likely to restrain Chinese decision-makers contemplating a conventional first strike on US forces and bases throughout the Western Pacific?

If PLA planners believe that the US would respect territorial 'firebreaks' or that it would be constrained by fear of escalation, they may suspect that it would not respond to strikes on American forces at sea (and perhaps in bases located on foreign soil) with retaliatory attacks on the Chinese mainland. By contrast, US counter-attacks on PLAN forces at sea might appear more proportional, less risky and hence more plausible. Threatening to carry out such attacks should, therefore, be a more effective deterrent.

Chinese decision-makers probably assess the near-term costs of a maritime-denial campaign as being greater than those of a distant energy blockade, but less than a barrage of US conventional precision strikes against targets on the mainland. If war came suddenly, it might take weeks for American and allied forces to move into position and to begin sweeping the near seas for Chinese naval vessels and commercial shipping. The effects of such a campaign would also be cumulative, and more time would pass before they were fully felt. Rather than threatening to promptly blind and partially disarm Beijing, maritime denial would confront the regime with the prospect of steadily mounting pain. Chinese planners might believe that they could ride out a distant energy blockade, or offset its effects through a variety of measures, but it would be harder for them to come up with credible plans for coping with a total suspension of overseas trade. If they believed that the US had the capacity and the resolve to carry it out, and if they were uncertain of their ability to quickly win a war, this threat would, therefore, be a potent one.

Long-term competition

A maritime-denial strategy would set American and allied strengths against Chinese weaknesses, play on underlying fears of encirclement and attack from the sea, and encourage the expenditure of resources on capabilities that are largely defensive in nature. Like the threat of a distant blockade, a maritime-denial strategy would push China into areas of warfare in which its experience and expertise are, at present, quite limited. By contrast, because the threat may seem more urgent and because potential responses to it are closer at hand, it would likely also impel Beijing to make choices and take action in the relatively near term. Visible US and allied preparations for a maritime-denial campaign could thus have considerable potential to shape the ongoing military competition.

In the words of Lyle Goldstein, 'Chinese anti-submarine warfare (ASW) remains an Achilles' Heel of the otherwise highly methodical and quite remarkable evolution of Chinese naval power.'[40] To date, ASW has not been treated as a high-priority mission. The technical and operational problems it presents are notoriously difficult to solve and, in any event, in the early stages of China's build-up, the main threat of attack was seen to come not from enemy submarines, but rather from aircraft and surface vessels (especially aircraft carriers). These naturally became the focal points of China's evolving A2/AD network. The PLAN did not have many surface ships to protect it from submarine attack. Most of those it did possess could not operate effectively far beyond coastal waters and may not have been expected to survive for very long after firing their weapons at the start of a conflict.

Goldstein argues that the Chinese navy now recognises its weakness and 'appears to understand that a massive national effort will be required' to enhance its ASW capabilities.[41] It remains to be seen whether such an effort will be forthcoming. The growing size and expanding range of the PLAN surface fleet, and the fact that other regional powers are acquiring more and better submarines, provide an obvious impetus for this belated development. The apparent success of China's A2/AD programmes in countering threats from the air and the sea's surface has also helped to highlight the relative weakness of its defences against undersea attack. The prospect that the US and its allies may now seek to exploit this vulnerability by preparing to mount a maritime-denial campaign could serve as an additional stimulus for substantial new investments in this area.

China has begun to take steps towards assembling the elements of an ASW capability, but it has a long way to go. At this point, the PLAN has a very limited capacity to detect, track and destroy enemy submarines. Some reports suggest that it has laid down rudimentary acoustic detection networks across 'significant littoral areas of the East and South China Sea'.[42] The navy is described as showing a 'keen interest in submarine-deployed towed sonar arrays', and is working on a dedicated ASW surface combatant that will eventually be armed with anti-submarine torpedoes and depth charges.[43] Although China presently has only a handful of fixed-wing aircraft and helicopters suitable for ASW missions, in late 2011 it reportedly unveiled a new variant of its Y-8 transport aircraft, equipped with sensors designed to detect submarines.[44] Perhaps to compensate for its shortcomings in more conventional techniques, the PLAN has shown a particular interest in defensive underwater mine barriers to keep enemy submarines out of protected areas.[45]

Responding to an enhanced threat from existing US and allied submarines will require considerable additional investments in all of the systems described above, as well as in the weaponry and training required to turn some Chinese submarines into effective ASW platforms. Smaller, more numerous, more difficult to detect and, above all, expendable, US and allied UUVs, capable of laying mines and attacking enemy ships, as well as submarines, would compound the difficulties confronting the PLAN. If the US decides to exploit the potential of UUVs, even as China's navy begins to acquire the capacity to cope with an existing challenge, it will find itself confronted by new ones against which it is even more difficult to defend.

Reassurance

Because it could be interpreted as conveying aggressive intent, being seen to prepare for a maritime-denial campaign could cause some unease among Washington's allies. On the other hand, the measures that those countries are already taking to enhance their own security – building or buying submarines, maritime-patrol aircraft, anti-ship missiles, unmanned aerial vehicles and improved command-and-control systems – are precisely what would be needed to assist in implementing a maritime-denial strategy.[46] While Beijing may not like what its neighbours are doing, its own build-up weakens the credibility of its objections.

Like ASB, a maritime-denial strategy calls for the US to be prepared to fight its way back into waters within the first island chain, even after having absorbed a first strike on its forward bases and forces. In contrast to the imposition of a distant blockade, this strategy would not leave China in control of its near seas. At a minimum, this approach would seek to create a zone of mutual denial, preventing Beijing from seizing and holding islands, conducting coastal shipping or exploiting undersea resources. If successful, US and allied operations would clear the way for the recapture of lost territory and the resumption of friendly commercial traffic. To the extent that the United States' regional partners have doubts about Washington's determination to restore the *status quo ante* – perhaps willing to sacrifice some of its allies' interests rather than risk a direct military confrontation with China – a maritime-denial strategy should help to allay their concerns.

Implications

As part of a maritime-denial strategy, the US would focus scarce resources on augmenting its existing capabilities for undersea warfare. Aside from building more nuclear-powered attack submarines, this could be done by adding a contingent of comparatively inexpensive diesel boats, or investing more heavily in UUVs. Hughes estimates that, for the price of one nuclear submarine, the navy could add as many as five diesels. Quiet and comparatively small, diesels would seem to be ideally suited to operations against Chinese submarines, surface combatants and commercial shipping in the Yellow Sea and the East and South China seas. However, as Hughes notes, they are 'at their best when they do not have to travel long distances to the scene of the action', so these submarines would have to be based forward (presumably in Japan, but perhaps also in the Philippines), or able to deploy rapidly to the theatre in the event of a crisis.[47]

After decades of exclusive reliance on nuclear propulsion, going back to building and operating diesel submarines would require dramatic transformations in the US Navy's long-standing organisational culture and existing industrial base. For these reasons, renewed investment in diesel submarines is highly unlikely.[48] By contrast, the navy appears to have enthusiastically embraced the potential of UUVs, and is experimenting with a variety of prototypes that could eventually conduct reconnaissance, deploy mines, fire torpedoes and lurk outside enemy ports. Assuming that limitations in existing techniques for energy storage and underwater communication can be overcome, UUVs promise to provide dramatic enhancements in combat capability at comparatively low cost.[49]

In light of the limited numbers of submarines available, the effectiveness and chances for success of a maritime-denial strategy would be greatly enhanced by the use of mines.[50] These could be deployed in order to seal ports to commercial traffic, and to sink enemy submarines and surface vessels attempting to travel between their bases and the near seas, or through the first island chain into the open ocean beyond. For a variety of reasons, however, the navy is extremely ill prepared for the conduct of either offensive or defensive mine warfare. Stockpiles of these weapons have been allowed to dwindle over the years, as has the capacity for their domestic manufacture. A 2005 report by the Naval Research Advisory Committee concluded that US mine-warfare capabilities were 'limited and rapidly dying', and despite some signs of increased interest, little has been done to reverse this trend.[51] The US Navy no longer has the capacity to lay mines with surface ships, and its submarine-launched mobile mines recently reached the end of their service life. The navy does have a limited supply of weapons that can be sown from the air, but none of the platforms that are equipped and train for this mission (the F/A-18, the B-52 and the B-1B) are stealthy enough to survive for long in an A2/AD environment.[52] While B-2s could conceivably be used in this role, they have limited payloads, are few in number and are likely to be in high demand for the performance of other top-priority missions. If the US chooses to pursue a maritime-denial strategy, it will have to invest more heavily in acquiring mines and survivable delivery systems, as well as working closely with allies, such as Japan, that retain significant capabilities in mine warfare.[53]

Notes

[1] For a comprehensive analysis, see Sean Mirski, 'Stranglehold: The Context, Conduct and Consequences of an American Naval Blockade of China', *Journal of Strategic Studies*, vol. 36, no. 3, June 2013.

[2] For a discussion of the role of land-based anti-ship cruise missiles in reinforcing a distant blockade, see Terence K. Kelly et al., *Employing Land-Based Anti-Ship Missiles in the Western Pacific* (Santa Monica, CA: RAND Corporation, 2013). Such weapons would only be useful in a 'hot' war in which the US and its allies were willing to sink commercial vessels attempting to run a blockade.

[3] Marc Lanteigne, 'China's Maritime Security and the "Malacca Dilemma"', *Asian Security*, vol. 4, no. 2, 2008, p. 150.

[4] Douglas C. Peifer, 'China, the German Analogy and the New AirSea Operational Concept', *Orbis*, vol. 55, no. 1, Winter 2011, p. 126.

[5] Robert Potter, 'The Importance of the Straits of Malacca', e-International Relations, 7 September 2012, http://www.e-ir.info/2012/09/07/the-importance-of-the-straits-of-malacca/.

[6] Peifer, 'China, the German Analogy and the New AirSea Operational Concept', p. 114.

[7] Gabriel B. Collins and William S. Murray, 'No Oil for the Lamps of China?', *Naval War College Review*, vol. 61, no. 2, Spring 2008, pp. 81–3.

[8] Roughly 165 vessels pass through the Malacca Strait each day, of which nearly one-third are oil tankers. Jason Glab, 'Blockading China: A Guide', *War On the Rocks*, 1 October 2013, http://warontherocks.com/2013/10/blockading-china-a-guide/.

[9] Such considerations would presumably weigh more heavily on American policymakers if they were contemplating making the first move rather than looking for ways to respond to Chinese attacks on US forces or those of its treaty allies. On these issues, see *ibid.*, pp. 83–6. For a response, see Peifer, 'China, the German Analogy and the New AirSea Operational Concept', pp. 127–9. Sean Mirski

suggests a number of ways in which a distant blockade could be made more effective, including the mandatory installation of 'digital navcerts', tamper-proof devices that would record a ship's movements and could be checked as they passed through checkpoints. Vessels that resisted tagging would be seized, along with those that were found to have broken the blockade and called at Chinese ports during a previous journey. Mirski, 'Stranglehold', pp. 404–7.

10 Collins and Murray, 'No Oil for the Lamps of China?', p. 87.

11 Having made this estimate, the authors conclude that precisely because the impact would be so large, putting national survival at stake, 'Chinese security planners may confidently discount completely the plausibility of a deliberate US oil blockade *under circumstances short of war.*' (Emphasis added.) Unless they believe that a war with the US is impossible, it is unlikely that Chinese planners find this at all reassuring. See Bruce Blair, Chen Yali and Eric Hagt, 'The Oil Weapon: Myth of China's Vulnerability', *China Security*, Summer 2006, pp. 53–4.

12 Mirski, 'Stranglehold', p. 413. Noting the methodological limitations of this estimate, Mirski concludes that it 'likely underestimates the short-term impact of an oil shortage while overstating its long-term economic effects'.

13 For overviews of this topic, see Chen Shaofeng, 'China's Self-Extrication from the "Malacca Dilemma" and Implications', *International Journal of China Studies*, vol. 1, no. 1, January 2010, pp. 1–24; ZhongXiang Zhang,

'China's energy security, the Malacca dilemma and responses', *Energy Policy*, no. 39, 2011, pp. 7,612–15.

14 Andrew S. Erickson and Gabriel B. Collins, 'China's Oil Security Pipe Dream: The Reality, and Strategic Consequences, of Seaborne Imports', *Naval War College Review*, vol. 63, no. 2, Spring 2010, p. 90.

15 For a discussion of the various projects and proposals, see *ibid.* A pipeline to bring oil from Burma to Yunnan Province was first proposed in 2004 and was scheduled to go into service in May 2013, along with a parallel line carrying natural gas. Teddy Ng, 'China–Myanmar Oil Pipe to Open in May', *South China Morning Post*, 22 January 2013, http://www.scmp.com/news/china/article/1133322/china-myanmar-oil-pipe-open-may. Proposals for a pipeline across Pakistan surfaced in 2006, but the idea seems to have been derailed by concerns over the country's political stability.

16 A comparison of projected demand with the estimated capacity of planned pipelines from Russia, Myanmar and Central Asia suggests that, by 2030, China may be able to obtain 15% of the oil it needs and 30% of its required natural gas via land routes. See Aaron L. Friedberg, 'Closing the Interest-Capabilities Gap: China's Possible Long-Term Objectives in the Near Seas', Long-Term Strategy Group, July 2011, pp. 6–8.

17 See Daniel J. Kostecka, 'Places and Bases: The Chinese Navy's Emerging Support Network in the Indian Ocean', *Naval War College Review*, vol. 64, no. 1, Winter

2011, pp. 59–78; Gabe Collins and Andrew Erickson, 'Implications of China's Military Evacuation of Citizens from Libya', *China Brief*, vol. 11, no. 4, 10 March 2011, http://www.jamestown.org/programs/chinabrief/single/?tx_ttnews%5Btt_news%5D=37633&cHash=7278cfd21e6fb19afe8a823c5cf88f07.

18 Such changes are conceivable, even if none seems imminent. If it opens sufficiently wide channels through the polar ice, global warming could enable oil from Africa and the Persian Gulf to reach China without transiting the narrow straits of Southeast Asia. Even if such shipments were possible, however, they would have to pass though the Atlantic, within easy reach of American naval power. Like the US, China is believed to have large continental deposits of shale oil and natural gas. For a variety of reasons, however, including a scarcity of water needed for 'fracking', it may be difficult to exploit these reserves. The most promising avenue for China to reduce its reliance on long-distance imports in the relatively near term is through gaining control over the vast oil and natural-gas deposits that are thought to lie beneath the East and South China seas. These might not be affected by a distant blockade but would be vulnerable to interdiction if the US and its allies pursued a strategy of maritime denial along the lines described in the next section.

19 This quote is from a 2009 article by Ye Hailin of the Chinese Academy of Social Sciences. Toshi Yoshihara and James R. Holmes, *Red Star Over the Pacific: China's Rise and the Challenge to US Maritime Strategy* (Annapolis, MD: Naval Institute Press, 2010), p. 20.

20 This discussion is drawn from Friedberg, 'Closing the Interest-Capabilities Gap', p. 5.

21 Whatever their contribution to a distant blockade, anti-ship missiles and other anti-access weapons would give friends and allies a greater capacity to defend themselves from an initial Chinese assault, even if the bulk of US forces were otherwise engaged. For proposals along these lines, see William S. Murray, 'Revisiting Taiwan's Defense Strategy', *Naval War College Review*, vol. 61, no. 3, Summer 2008, pp. 13–38; and Toshi Yoshihara, 'Japan's Competitive Strategies at Sea: A Preliminary Assessment', in Thomas G. Mahnken (ed.), *Competitive Strategies for the 21st Century: Theory, History, and Practice* (Stanford, CA: Stanford University Press, 2012), pp. 219–35.

22 Mirski, 'Stranglehold', p. 408.

23 See Jeffrey E. Kline and Wayne P. Hughes, Jr, 'Between Peace and the Air-Sea Battle: A War at Sea Strategy', *Naval War College Review*, vol. 65, no. 4, Autumn 2012, pp. 35–40; T.X. Hammes, 'Offshore Control: A Proposed Strategy for an Unlikely Conflict', *Strategic Forum*, no. 278, June 2012; Michael Raska, 'Decoding the Air-Sea Battle Concept: Operational Consequences and Allied Concerns', *RSIS Commentaries*, no. 158/2012, 23 August 2012; and Raoul Heinrichs, 'America's Dangerous Battle Plan', *Diplomat*, 17 August 2011, http://thediplomat.com/2011/08/17/america's-dangerous-battle-plan.

24 On the utility of coastal combatants, see Kline and Hughes, 'Between Peace and the Air-Sea Battle: A War at Sea Strategy', pp. 37–8. The possible role of land-based ASCMs is discussed in Toshi Yoshihara and James R. Holmes, 'Asymmetric Warfare, American Style', *US Naval Institute Proceedings*, vol. 138, no. 4, April 2012, pp. 24–9.

25 Kline and Hughes, 'Between Peace and the Air-Sea Battle', p. 39.

26 China Trade Profile, World Trade Organization, September 2013, http://stat.wto.org/CountryProfile/WSDBCountryPFView.aspx?Country=CN&.

27 Dean Cheng, 'Sea Power and the Chinese State: China's Maritime Ambitions', *Heritage Foundation Backgrounder*, no. 2576, July 2011, p. 1.

28 Yoshihara and Holmes, 'Asymmetric Warfare'.

29 The technical issues are summarised and explained in Owen R. Cote, Jr, 'Assessing the Undersea Balance Between the US and China', MIT Security Studies Program Working Paper, February 2011, pp. 4–8. On the PLAN's recent efforts to correct some of its shortcomings, see Lyle Goldstein, 'Beijing Confronts Long-Standing Weaknesses in Anti-Submarine Warfare', *China Brief*, vol. 11, no. 14, 29 July 2011.

30 Ronald O'Rourke, *Navy Virginia (SSN-774) Class Attack Submarine Procurement: Background and Issues for Congress* (Washington DC: Congressional Research Service, 2012), p. 9.

31 Japan Ministry of Defense, *Defense of Japan 2012* (Tokyo: Japan Ministry of Defense, 2012), p. 131.

32 'South Korea Submarine Capabilities', Nuclear Threat Initiative, 13 July 2013, http://www.nti.org/analysis/articles/south-korea-submarine-capabilities/.

33 'Australia Submarine Capabilities', Nuclear Threat Initiative, 15 July 2013, http://www.nti.org/analysis/articles/australia-submarine-capabilities/.

34 Cote, *Assessing the Undersea Balance Between the US and China*, p. 3.

35 Wayne P. Hughes, *The New Navy Fighting Machine: A Study of the Connections Between Contemporary Policy, Strategy, Sea Power, Naval Operations, and the Composition of the United States Fleet* (Monterey, CA: Naval Postgraduate School, 2009), p. 36.

36 Kline and Hughes, 'Between Peace and the Air-Sea Battle', p. 37. Jan van Tol identifies a similar goal and describes the necessary elements of a successful campaign. Unlike Hughes, however, he assumes that the US would also conduct attacks on the Chinese mainland that would support its ability to eventually establish control of the near seas. Jan van Tol et al., *AirSea Battle: A Point-of-Departure Operational Concept* (Washington DC: Center for Strategic and Budgetary Assessments, 2010), pp. 71–4.

37 Hammes, 'Offshore Control', p. 10.

38 Bernard Cole, 'China's Naval Modernization: Cause for Storm Warnings?', National Defense University, 16 June 2010.

39 Michael Pillsbury, 'The Sixteen Fears: China's Strategic Psychology', *Survival*, vol. 54, no. 5, October–November 2012, pp. 152–3.

40 Goldstein, 'Beijing Confronts Long-Standing Weaknesses in Anti-Submarine Warfare'.

41 *Ibid.*

42 Van Tol, *AirSea Battle*, p. 26.

43 Goldstein, 'Beijing Confronts Long-Standing Weaknesses in Anti-Submarine Warfare'.

44 Claire Apthorp, 'Anti-Submarine Warfare: ASW Capabilities in the Asian Region', *Defence Review Asia*, 19 March 2012, http://www.defence reviewasia.com/articles/155/ Anti-Submarine-Warfare.

45 Goldstein, 'Beijing Confronts Long-Standing Weaknesses in Anti-Submarine Warfare'.

46 For an overview of regional developments, see Geoffrey Till, *Asia's Naval Expansion: An Arms Race in the Making?*, Adelphi 432–33 (London: Routledge for the International Institute for Strategic Studies, 2012).

47 Hughes, Jr, *The New Navy Fighting Machine*, p. 36.

48 Hughes advocates doubling the size of the navy's fleet of attack submarines by building a force of at least 40 diesel-powered boats. *Ibid.*, pp. 35–8. For a summary of the arguments in favour of this option, see Gary J. Schmitt, 'US Navy Needs Diesel Submarines', *Defense News*, 12 June 2011, http://www. defensenews.com/article/20110612/ DEFFEAT05/106120303/U-S-Navy-Needs-Diesel-Submarines. American naval yards stopped building diesel attack submarines in 1959. Norman Polmar, *The Naval Institute Guide to the Ships and Aircraft of the US Fleet* (Annapolis, MD: US Naval Institute, 2005), pp. 88–9.

49 On the potential of UUVs, see Edward C. Whitman, 'Unmanned Underwater Vehicles: Beneath the Wave of the Future', *Undersea Warfare*, no. 15, http://www. navy.mil/navydata/cno/n87/usw/ issue_15/wave.html; Scott Pratt, 'Asymmetric and Affordable', *US Naval Institute Proceedings*, vol. 138, no. 6, June 2012, pp. 46–9; Naval Research Advisory Committee, 'How Autonomy Can Transform Naval Operations', October 2012, http://www.nrac.navy.mil/docs/ NRAC_Final_Report-Autonomy_ NOV2012.pdf.

50 Mirski describes this somewhat optimistically as the 'one exception to the readiness of the United States' current and programmed force structure' to implement a blockade strategy. Mirski, 'Stranglehold', p. 409.

51 Scott C. Truver, 'Taking Mines Seriously: Mine Warfare in China's Near Seas', *Naval War College Review*, vol. 65, no. 2, Spring 2012, p. 57.

52 *Ibid.*, pp. 53–7.

53 Toshi Yoshihara points out that the Japan Maritime Self-Defense Force possesses 'a world-class minesweeping fleet that could be refitted and retrained for laying mines'. Yoshihara, 'Japan's Competitive Strategies at Sea', p. 227.

Whatever its eventual dimensions, the American response to China's anti-access/area-denial (A2/AD) challenge will involve a blend of direct and indirect approaches. The United States will likely enhance its capabilities for striking at least some targets on China's mainland, while also strengthening its capacity to wage war in the waters off China's coast. Because US planners must pursue an array of objectives, including deterrence, reassurance, preparations for war and the conduct of a long-term competition, they will have to satisfice, selecting a mixture of policies that serve disparate purposes, rather than pursuing what might be the optimal solution to a more straightforward military problem. Non-strategic factors will also shape, and may distort, US strategy, including long-standing preferences within the armed services for certain weapons and approaches to war fighting; inter-service rivalry; and, at least in the near-to-medium term, persistent downward pressure on defence spending.

Elements of a strategy

Proponents of Air–Sea Battle (ASB), maritime denial and a distant blockade generally agree on the importance of three things: reducing the vulnerability of US forces and bases to conventional precision strikes; the leverage that can be obtained by threatening to constrict China's maritime energy-supply lines; and the virtues of coordinating closely with friendly countries. Where their views differ is on the extent to which the US and its allies should be prepared to conduct offensive operations inside the first island chain, and possibly against the Chinese mainland. Because their focus is on conventional warfare, advocates of all three approaches tend to ignore or downplay the role of nuclear weapons.

Reducing vulnerability

There is little disagreement that the US and its allies need to do what they can to reduce the confidence of People's Liberation Army (PLA) planners in their ability to carry out a successful conventional first strike. This is most clearly the case for proponents of ASB, who identify the defence of forward-based forces and facilities as both a core objective and an essential precondition for operational success. While it is conceivable that a distant blockade or maritime denial could be implemented in the aftermath of a devastating strike on bases, satellites, command, control, communication, computers, intelligence, surveillance and reconnaissance (C4ISR) networks and surface combatants, it would be harder to sustain the necessary operations if they had to be mounted from outside the 'threat rings' of China's A2/AD forces (see p. 30, Chapter One).

Reducing vulnerability will require continuing investment in a mixture of active and passive measures: missile and air defences; hardening; redundancy in cyber networks, satellites and C4ISR systems; dispersal within the theatre; and the relocation of some critical assets outside the range of China's missiles. Cover and deception operations may also be useful, helping to reduce the opponent's confidence in peacetime about the likely performance of its forces, and increasing uncertainty in a crisis about the location of key targets. In addition to determining the aggregate level of spending on defensive measures, as compared to other elements in an overall strategy, American and allied planners will have to make choices regarding the precise blend of active and passive defences, the balance between investment in existing kinetic-kill systems and as yet unproven directed-energy weapons, and the extent to which limited funds should be spent on increasing the reliability of C4ISR networks.[1]

Eliminating vulnerability is obviously impossible and, from a strategic standpoint, unnecessary and even undesirable. Throughout the Cold War, American forward-based forces and facilities were exposed to the danger of Soviet pre-emption, and some of them would no doubt have been damaged or destroyed at the start of a war. Precisely for this reason, the placement of these assets contributed to deterrence. Accepting a measure of vulnerability could help to make clear to Chinese decision-makers that if they attack its allies, they will be at war with the US.

Maintaining the threat of an energy blockade

Cutting off Chinese energy imports is the central goal of a distant blockade. While they do not consider it sufficient in itself, the proponents of a more thoroughgoing maritime-denial strategy have no objection, in principle, to interdicting oil tankers at key choke points. Some see such operations and those within the South and East China seas as complementary parts of a single strategy.[2] Even many ASB advocates, acknowledging that the defeat of China's A2/AD systems would not be sufficient to win a war in itself, favour imposing a distant blockade as part of a second phase in what could well prove to be a protracted conflict.[3]

Even if they tried, it is extremely unlikely that US policy-makers could persuade Beijing that they have no intention of ever exploiting China's dependence on imported energy. That threat is an unavoidable by-product of the prevailing balance of maritime power and, notwithstanding impending shifts in US and Chinese naval capabilities, will not disappear anytime soon. The question facing US planners is whether, together with a handful of allies, they should make a series of small and comparatively inexpensive gestures that would keep this prospect front and centre in Chinese minds.[4] The advantage of doing so is that the threat of a distant blockade could contribute to deterrence, while at the same time encouraging China to continue diverting scarce resources away from more menacing purposes. This would be the case regardless of its actual impact on the outcome of a future war.

Such a conclusion comes with an important caveat. In a crisis situation, if Chinese decision-makers actually believed economic strangulation was imminent, they would be more likely to risk aggression or escalation. Beginning to put pressure on energy supplies in the hopes of persuading Beijing to alter course in a crisis could, therefore, be more dangerous than merely alluding to the possibility in peacetime. It would be especially dangerous if Chinese planners thought that they could alleviate their vulnerability through decisive military action, perhaps by seizing and securing oil- and gas-production facilities in the South and East China seas.

Developing offensive options
Long-range precision strike
A purely defensive strategy, while perhaps appealing to those who fear being unnecessarily provocative, does not adequately fulfil the requirements of deterrence, war fighting, reassurance and the long-term military competition. Of the three alterna-

tives, the distant-blockade strategy comes closest to the ideal of a non-provocative defence, but even many advocates of the concept envision it being implemented in conjunction with other, more aggressive operations. Whatever the merits of staying on the defensive, as James FitzSimonds points out, American military officers have a deeply ingrained aversion to approaches to warfare that they regard as excessively passive, or tantamount to 'doing nothing'.[5]

In reality, the toughest choices facing military planners concern not whether, but how, and how aggressively, to threaten or take the offensive against China. The first dividing line in the debate over this issue is between the advocates of maritime denial, who seek to avoid strikes against targets on the Chinese mainland, and the proponents of ASB, who believe that a war cannot be won without such attacks.

The reluctance of some analysts to contemplate strikes on Chinese territory is understandable, but only up to a point. They argue that even threatening to carry them out might raise the risk of instability in a crisis; actually doing so could result in rapid escalation, and even the possibility of a nuclear exchange. Regardless of the possible military advantages, no American president is likely to implement such strikes prior to a major Chinese provocation.[6] Should China initiate an A2/AD campaign, however, these inhibitions would weaken, and could dissolve altogether. If the PLA launches a first strike against US and allied forces and bases, failing to respond in kind would mean granting it a sanctuary from which to conduct reconnaissance and follow-on attacks. Having absorbed an initial blow, it is difficult to see how the US and its allies could reconstitute their forces and go on the offensive without, at a minimum, taking steps to disrupt China's C4ISR networks. Military considerations aside, allied leaders would also face enormous political pressure to, as James Holmes puts it, 'retaliate against the source of attacks on their ships, their sons, and their daughters'.[7]

Abstaining from preparations for attacks on the Chinese mainland could also weaken deterrence and put the US at a serious disadvantage in the long-term military competition. Chinese leaders who do not fear prompt, proportionate retaliation for conventional strikes on US and allied forces and bases may underestimate the risks of starting a war. If they believe that their opponents have lost the capacity and resolve to strike the mainland, PLA planners will feel free to shift resources away from defences, towards building up their offensive capabilities.

At present, the US does have some capacity to launch precision conventional strikes on China and, despite the absence of a clear-cut consensus on strategy, is in the process of acquiring a greater capacity to do so. The question confronting American planners is a familiar one: how much is enough? More specifically: what range of targets should US forces be prepared to hit, and with what kinds of delivery systems should these attacks be carried out? At one extreme, the target list could include everything from hardened underground facilities located deep in the Chinese interior to large numbers of mobile, conventional missile launchers roaming the countryside. At the other end of the spectrum, the US might choose to concentrate on a relatively small number of critical targets, many of which are comparatively soft: over-the-horizon (OTH) radars, space-launch facilities, satellite-downlink stations and a handful of key nodes in China's C4ISR network.

For purposes of deterrence, war fighting, and shaping the long-term competition, the US should seek to acquire the capability to conduct quick, blinding strikes on the C4ISR installations that support China's A2/AD forces. It would also be desirable to be able to hold at risk, with conventional weapons, an array of targets: some that were soft and close to the coast (including airfields and ports), others located deep inside China (including space-launch facilities and OTH radars) and still others that were hardened. While having the ability to go after at least some mobile targets might also appear attractive, the benefits of being able to locate, track and destroy hundreds of them across the length and breadth of China, as some advocates of ASB seem to suggest, are not sufficient to justify the costs.

The weapons systems that the Pentagon is presently procuring – F-35s, more extended-range air-to-surface missiles and possibly more submarine-launched cruise missiles – are useful for hitting fixed, and at least some mobile, targets within a few hundred miles of China's eastern seaboard. US forces currently have a limited capacity to strike deep using B-2 penetrating bombers. While several other systems in development could perform these missions, some (for example, a follow-on manned bomber) have long development timelines and others (such as hypersonic boost-glide vehicles) rely on technologies that are as yet unproven. Because the services' preferred platforms for delivering conventional munitions are so expensive, and budgets are so tight, less money is likely to be available for developing alternatives that could provide capability quickly and at relatively low cost.[8] One such option, a submarine-launched, conventional ballistic missile, has encountered stiff opposition from a cost-conscious Congress.[9]

Retaining the ability to conduct strikes with air-breathing systems, while adding the capacity to do so using ballistic missiles (or more exotic hypersonic boost-glide vehicles), would complicate the PLA's planning and reinforce its inclination to expend resources on active and passive defences against both modes of attack. Very high-speed, non-air-breathing systems (rocket-launched hypersonic glide vehicles, as well as ballistic missiles), and possibly hypersonic cruise missiles, would allow the US to threaten prompt retaliation for a Chinese first strike while reducing the effectiveness of possible follow-on attacks.[10]

In addition to developing conventional ballistic missiles and continuing to explore other possibilities for executing prompt long-range strikes, the air force and navy need to change their mixture of manned and unmanned air-breathing systems. Given the importance of the Asian theatre, with its vast distances, investing large sums in manned aircraft that have a limited unrefuelled range and fly from vulnerable bases is not a wise investment. Some of this money would be better spent on developing and procuring more longer-range air- and sea-launched cruise missiles, long-endurance unmanned aerial vehicles of various types and, in the somewhat longer term, a new manned penetrating bomber.

Undersea warfare

Maritime denial is not incompatible with ASB. While the US might, out of concern about escalation, choose to conduct a war at sea without striking targets on land, if it did decide to carry out attacks on the Chinese mainland, there would be little reason for it to refrain from also sinking ships and submarines. Indeed, the two campaigns could be complementary. Strikes on airfields, ports and C4ISR facilities would limit the People's Liberation Army Navy's (PLAN) ability to contest control of the South and East China seas. Meanwhile, effective naval operations could reduce the risks to US and allied surface combatants and submarines, enabling them to operate closer to China's coasts and to conduct more effective strikes against targets on land.

As with ASB, the US already has some of the capabilities needed to implement a maritime-denial strategy. Here too, the relevant question is not whether, but how, to enhance its capacity to carry out the kinds of military operations necessary to support the strategy. The US Navy has an impressive fleet of highly capable nuclear-attack submarines and long experience in the coordination of air, surface and subsea assets for purposes of anti-submarine warfare (ASW). If American planners want to pursue a maritime-denial strategy, however, they will have to supplement the forces available for blockading Chinese ports and sinking PLAN surface ships and submarines. In addition to working with allies, there are two ways of doing this, only one of which appears to have generated any enthusiasm among planners.

Like their aerial counterparts, unmanned underwater vehicles (UUVs) can maintain coverage of a wide range of targets for an extended period of time, leaving manned assets free to conduct other high-priority missions. The combination of US and allied submarines and UUVs would pose a potent threat to Chinese shipping and press the PLAN to increase its investment in ASW, an area of long-standing weakness. Unmanned vehicles are a central part of the US Navy's vision of future warfare. According to the chief of naval operations, over the next decade and a half, the navy will deploy a 'family' of UUVs of various sizes that will help it to 'sustain the undersea dominance that is a clear US asymmetric advantage'.[11] Among the systems being fielded are a Persistent Littoral Undersea Surveillance network that sits 'on the ocean floor listening to undersea contacts and sending its results back (in real time) via an unmanned vehicle and satellite link', and a '20-foot long, 5-foot diameter vessel which can autonomously travel hundreds of miles and operate for weeks or months' without human intervention.[12]

Mines (some of which more closely resemble UUVs than the traditional tethered underwater device) could add an additional layer of complexity to the problems facing Chinese planners. However, for a variety of reasons, the US Navy has devoted very little money or energy to the development of these weapons. According to James FitzSimonds, although there have been proposals for new mobile mines that could be delivered by submarines or aircraft operating at safe distances from China's coasts, 'there has been no concrete action to upgrade the US mine inventory – or to bring mining into the mainstream of military planning and operations.' As a result, and despite the growing threat from Chinese mines, the US 'presents no comparable capability either to deter China or to divert China's military resources'.[13] If it is serious about maritime denial, the US Navy will need to address this shortfall.

Coordinating with allies

As China's capabilities continue to grow, preserving a favourable Asian balance of power will require more effort and closer coordination among the US and its regional partners. Whatever strategy they adopt, American planners will want to encourage other countries to take steps to reduce their vulnerability to sudden attack and to assist the US in doing the same by hardening, dispersing and defending its forward-based forces. To the extent that allies can contribute to the defence of their own territory, airspace and maritime approaches, this will help to reduce the burden on US forces. Certain kinds of systems, including land-, air- and sea-launched anti-ship cruise missiles, submarines, mines and ASW aircraft and surface vessels, could be helpful in imposing a distant blockade. Depending on their range and the location of their bases, some of these could also participate in maritime-denial operations.

American planners will likely be more ambivalent about encouraging others to develop their own long-range, conventional precision-strike capabilities. On the one hand, if they can hit targets in China, these could help US allies to deter similar attacks on themselves. At the same time, the proliferation of such systems could increase the risk that others may take steps leading to escalation, enhance mutual suspicions in allied capitals (most notably Seoul, which already has ballistic- and cruise-missile capabilities, and Tokyo), and divert scarce resources from more useful and less problematic investments.

The nuclear dimension

The debate over US strategy has thus far focused almost exclu- sively on conventional forces. ASB advocates generally put nuclear weapons to one side either obliquely (by acknowl- edging that their preferred approach deals with only a limited range of potential contingencies) or explicitly (by assuming, for planning purposes, that a conflict will remain limited to the conventional level).[14] Meanwhile, the proponents of maritime denial and a distant blockade argue that their proposals are motivated precisely by the desire to reduce the risk of nuclear escalation.

Whatever approach theorists might prefer, nuclear weapons will loom large over any future conflict and US planners have no choice but to address their role.[15] There are two sets of issues that demand attention. ASB critics have worried that attacks on the Chinese mainland might provoke escalation, but there has been little discussion of what, if anything, can be done to deter such a response. Part of the answer will presumably have to do with the size and structure of US nuclear forces, as well as the availability of credible options for their use. In the extremely unlikely event that the Sino-American nuclear balance shifts to the point at which China's leaders believe they could carry out an effective first strike on US nuclear forces, the risks of an esca- latory response to ASB-type attacks would rise considerably. At the other extreme, if, through some combination of offensive and defensive measures, the US could put itself in a position to sharply limit damage from a nuclear attack, the dangers of deliberate Chinese escalation would presumably dwindle. Assuming that neither side can be confident of destroying the other's capacity for nuclear retaliation, American planners will still need to prepare options with which to respond to limited nuclear use by China. If Chinese decision-makers are contemplating the demonstrative use of nuclear weapons against a small number of US and allied targets, or a detonation in space, intended to both demonstrate resolve and damage communications systems with an electromagnetic pulse, they should know that the US is prepared to respond in kind.

The final, and in some ways more difficult, question is when (if ever) and how the US might initiate the use of nuclear weapons in response to a Chinese conventional first strike. As discussed in Chapter Three, the threat of escalation is implicit in existing US security guarantees and is underlined by the fact that Washington has consistently refused to follow China's lead in issuing a no-first-use pledge. At a minimum, whatever they have to say about the possible long-term goal of eliminating nuclear weapons, future administrations should continue to adhere to this position. Beyond this, Washington needs to make clear, through its declaratory policy and force posture, that, in the event of a sufficiently large and devastating conventional attack, it might have little choice but to retaliate with nuclear weapons. Despite their formal policy, this is precisely what Chinese spokesmen have been signalling in some of their recent comments. Such threats may be of questionable credibility but, to the extent that they sow doubt in the minds of an opponent's decision-makers, can contribute to deterrence.

Under-examined issues
Protracted, high-intensity warfare
Assuming that it had not begun accidentally, a Sino-American military clash could drag on for months or even years. This

would certainly be the case if the US adopted a blockade strategy of some type. It could also be true in a scenario in which the two combatants traded cyber attacks and rapid volleys of missiles, as envisioned in their respective operational concepts. Even if the outcome of these initial exchanges was lopsided, the winner of the early rounds would have succeeded only in wounding its opponent rather than depriving it of the capacity to wage war. The decision to carry on would therefore be a function of political will rather than military capability. And both sides would be highly motivated to continue the fight: for the US, the stakes would include its future position as an Asian power and the credibility of its alliance commitments; China's leaders, meanwhile, may see avoiding outright defeat as a matter of regime survival.

In his elucidation of ASB, Jan van Tol notes that, even if his recommendations were adopted, a 'Sino-US conventional conflict would likely devolve into a prolonged war'. To prevail in such a struggle, he suggests that the US would have to 'mobilize key parts of its own defense industrial base, particularly those concerned with volume production of long-range precision-guided munitions'.[16] Given the rates at which these munitions would be expended, this is surely correct. However, in a war in which planes were being shot down, satellites disabled and ships sunk, precision-guided munitions would only be the tip of a very large iceberg. Replacing major weapons platforms would involve a mobilisation of industrial capacity unlike anything in which the US has engaged in over half a century. This, in turn, would require overcoming problems of administration and production to which virtually no serious thought has been given since the late 1970s and early 1980s, when the US Department of Defense (DoD) briefly wrestled with the prospect of a protracted conventional war against the Soviet Union.[17]

Because it inevitably calls for the diversion of resources from current capabilities to what are seen as wasteful preparations for very low-probability contingencies, mobilisation planning has no natural constituency within the armed forces. Aside from the possibility that they may actually have to be put into effect, the most compelling argument for such preparations is that they can contribute to deterrence. While they no doubt wish to avoid a long war at almost any cost, Chinese strategists may, nevertheless, believe that if a conflict drags on, China's large manufacturing base and state-planning apparatus could give them an edge. Visible American preparations for a protracted war could lessen confidence on this score, while forcing Chinese planners to contemplate the risks and dangers that will confront them if their hopes for a quick victory are not fulfilled.

Prospects for control

The growth of Chinese military power has led, in recent years, to a resurgence of interest in arms control, a topic that seemed to have lost much of its relevance with the end of the Cold War. Most of what has been written on this subject in the context of Sino-American relations has centred on either nuclear weapons or maritime confidence-building measures. In the first instance, US analysts have stressed the importance of avoiding an action–reaction cycle, in which a combination of US missile defences and conventional precision-strike weapons might stimulate an expansion in Chinese offensive nuclear forces. In the second instance, they have sought to devise measures that would reduce the risks of dangerous incidents at sea involving US and Chinese ships and aircraft.[18]

Compared to these issues, relatively little attention has thus far been paid to the possible role of negotiated agreements in limiting or channelling the emerging competition between

China's evolving A2/AD complex and US efforts to preserve its capacity for power projection. While a number of proposals have been advanced, none has any imminent prospect of being accepted as the basis for serious discussions. Some observers have suggested that the US (perhaps joined by Russia) should press for global adoption of the 1987 Intermediate-Range Nuclear Forces (INF) Treaty.[19] This agreement required the US and the Soviet Union to eliminate land-based ballistic and cruise missiles with ranges between 500km and 5,500km. If China were to follow suit, it would have to dismantle a significant portion of its conventional missile force, thereby lessening the threat to the US and its allies. The difficulty with this proposal is that, at least for the moment, there is nothing for Beijing to gain from it.[20] Perhaps if Chinese planners believed that the US was on the verge of deploying some new and very threatening capability – an extremely effective missile-defence system based on directed energy, for example, or a hypersonic global precision-strike platform – they might be willing to contemplate some limits on their own offensive forces. For the moment, however, there is no reason for them to trade existing weapons for future ones that are still on the drawing board.[21]

China's 2007 demonstration of an anti-satellite weapon (ASAT) prompted suggestions that the US agree to a treaty to prevent 'an arms race in outer space' or, at a minimum, press for a code of conduct that would restrict destructive, debris-producing ASAT tests.[22] Given its comparatively heavy reliance on space to conduct distant military operations, the US would seem to have much to gain from maintaining the status quo. However, a combination of doubts about the verifiability of an ASAT ban, confidence in US technological superiority, and a desire to preserve their own options have helped to make American military planners unenthusiastic about such proposals.[23] Chinese strategists, despite their loudly proclaimed opposition to the weaponisation of space, may be reluctant to forswear the opportunity to exploit what they see as an asymmetric American vulnerability. As China too becomes more dependent on space, this attitude may change, even as the further development of the PLA's anti-satellite capabilities could cause a reassessment of US policy. Unless the perceived interests of the two parties converge more closely than they do at present, there is little likelihood of meaningful agreements in this domain.

Cyberspace is one area in which both sides already have reason to feel vulnerable, and might therefore be willing to contemplate mutual restraints. As with outer space, there have recently been proposals for some kind of global treaty intended to constrain the offensive activities of all signatories, including the US and China.[24] Here too, there have been more modest suggestions for codes of conduct under which, at a minimum, the two nations would identify 'red lines' that, if crossed, could provoke or escalate conflict.[25] The reluctance of both powers to reveal or acknowledge their capabilities is a substantial obstacle, even to preliminary dialogue on this subject. Even if the two sides are willing to talk, it is not clear that they could agree on procedures to attribute responsibility for cyber attacks, nor is it apparent how meaningful sanctions could be imposed, especially if attacks occurred at the start of actual kinetic exchanges. The fact that there are, at present, no obvious answers to these questions does not mean that they are not worth pursuing.

Understanding Chinese assessments

The ultimate aim of American strategy is not to win a war with China, but to avoid ever having to fight one. For this purpose, nothing is more important than acquiring a better understanding of Chinese perceptions, assessments and decision-making processes. History suggests that the pay-offs from gaining such insight can be substantial. In the latter stages of the Cold War, the US and its allies were able to piece together a picture of how the Soviet Union assessed the NATO–Warsaw Pact military balance, and how it intended to fight and win a conventional conflict in Europe. Western analysts also gained a deeper understanding of how the Soviets planned to deploy their submarines in wartime. These insights were the by-product of several decades of intensive efforts at intelligence collection and analysis, and they fed directly into allied decisions about weapons, tactics and war planning. This culminated in the adoption of what came to be known as the Air–Land Battle doctrine and the Maritime Strategy. Shifts in strategy helped to bolster deterrence at a time when the Soviets appeared to be gaining a significant edge in conventional capabilities, and moved the ongoing military-technical competition in directions that favoured the US and its advanced industrial allies.[26] While it is unlikely, at this comparatively early stage in their rivalry, that the US has a similarly deep understanding of China, it should be working hard to acquire one.

Notes

[1] In part because their effectiveness may be enhanced by offensive action, defences will also have to be assessed as part of an overall US force posture and strategy. As Jan van Tol suggests, attacks on Chinese conventional ballistic-missile launchers could enhance the effectiveness of missile defences. Similarly, dispersed allied assets are more likely to survive if China loses its 'eyes' to a blinding attack.

[2] Sean Mirski, 'Stranglehold: The Context, Conduct and Consequences of an American Naval Blockade of China', *Journal of Strategic Studies*, vol. 36, no. 3, June 2013, pp. 385–421.

[3] See Jan van Tol et al., *AirSea Battle: A Point-of-Departure Operational Concept* (Washington DC: Center for Strategic and Budgetary Assessments, 2010), pp. 76–8.

[4] Allies might include Japan, Australia, the Philippines and perhaps also Singapore and Indonesia. The gestures could include exercises simulating various aspects of a distant blockade or intercepting and searching ships.

5   This point is made in the context of a discussion of the virtues of passive versus active missile defences, but it applies more generally. See James R. FitzSimonds, 'Cultural Barriers to Implementing a Competitive Strategy', in Thomas G. Mahnken (ed.), *Competitive Strategies for the 21st Century: Theory, History, and Practice* (Stanford, CA: Stanford University Press, 2012), p. 294.

6   Although the Chinese may not believe it, the ASB concept is explicitly premised on the assumption that the US will not strike first. ASBO, 'Air-Sea Battle: Service Collaboration to Address Anti-Access and Area Denial Challenges', May 2013, p. 3.

7   James R. Holmes, 'Airsea Battle VS Offshore Control: Can the US Blockade China?', *Diplomat*, 19 August 2013, http://thediplomat.com/the-naval-diplomat/2013/08/19/airsea-battle-vs-offshore-control-can-the-us-blockade-china/.

8   The costs and range limitations of F-35s and land-attack cruise missiles have already been discussed. For one possible alternative, and the military's resistance to it, see the discussion of the virtues of the Low Cost Autonomous Attack System in FitzSimonds, 'Cultural Barriers to Implementing a Competitive Strategy', p. 291.

9   See Elaine M. Grossman, 'Pentagon, Lawmakers Deal Blows to Navy Fast-Strike Missile Effort', Global Security Newswire, 31 July 2013, http://www.nti.org/gsn/article/pentagon-lawmakers-deal-blows-navy-fast-strike-missile-effort/. In addition to concerns over cost, some legislators worry that incoming US conventional ballistic missiles could be mistaken as the first wave of a pre-emptive nuclear strike, thereby triggering Chinese escalation.

10 On the various types of high-speed conventional weapons, see Amy F. Woolf, *Conventional Prompt Global Strike and Long-Range Ballistic Missiles: Background and Issues* (Washington DC: Congressional Research Service, 2013); and James M. Acton, *Silver Bullet? Asking the Right Questions About Prompt Global Strike* (Washington DC: Carnegie Endowment for International Peace, 2013).

11 Ronald O'Rourke, *China Naval Modernization: Implications for US Navy Capabilities – Background and Issues for Congress* (Washington DC: Congressional Research Service, 2013), p. 56.

12 Jonathan Greenert, 'How the US Can Maintain the Undersea Advantage', *Defense One*, 21 October 2013, http://www.defenseone.com/ideas/2013/10/how-us-can-maintain-undersea-advantage/72314/.

13 FitzSimonds, 'Cultural Barriers to Implementing a Competitive Strategy', p. 296.

14 The DoD's concept paper states that ASB is 'a limited but critical component in a spectrum of initiatives aimed at shaping the security environment'. ASBO, 'Air-Sea Battle', p. i. One of the 'critical assumptions' in the Center for Strategic and Budgetary Assessment's elaboration of the concept is that 'mutual nuclear deterrence holds'. Van Tol et al., *AirSea Battle*, p. 50.

15 The most comprehensive discussion of the possible interaction between conventional and nuclear forces to date is Avery Goldstein, 'First Things First: The Pressing Danger of Crisis Instability in US-China Relations', *International Security*, vol. 37, no. 4, Spring 2013, pp. 49–89.

16 Van Tol et al., *AirSea Battle*, pp. 31–2.

17 This episode is discussed in Aaron L. Friedberg, *In the Shadow of the Garrison State: America's Anti-Statism and its Cold War Grand Strategy* (Princeton, NJ: Princeton University Press, 2000), pp. 235–44.

18 Concern over both of these issues dates back to the late 1990s. For recent discussions, see PONI Working Group on US-China Nuclear Dynamics, *Nuclear Weapons and US-China Relations: A Way Forward* (Washington DC: Center for Strategic and International Studies, 2013); Philippe de Koning and Tong Zhao, 'The United States, China, and Nuclear Arms Control: Time for a Creative Spark', *PacNet Newsletter*, no. 63, 8 August 2013; David Griffiths, *US-China Maritime Confidence Building: Paradigms, Precedents, and Prospects* (Newport, RI: China Maritime Studies Institute, 2010); and David Gompert, 'How To Avert a Sea Catastrophe with China', *US News and World Report*, 6 May 2013.

19 See Mark A. Stokes and Ian Easton, *Evolving Aerospace Trends in the Asia-Pacific Region* (Washington DC: Project 2049 Institute, May 2010), pp. 36–8; Mark Stokes and Dan Blumenthal, 'Can a Treaty Contain China's Missiles?', *Washington Post*, 2 January 2011; Thomas Donnelly, 'American Zero', *Weekly Standard*, 4 June 2011, p. 11; David A. Cooper, 'Globalizing Reagan's INF Treaty: Easier Said Than Done?', *Nonproliferation Review*, vol. 20, no. 1, 2013, pp. 145–63.

20 Unsurprisingly, Chinese analysts reject proposals for the globalisation of the INF Treaty as being 'aimed at China'. See 'SCRAP Interview with Chinese Arms Control Expert Professor Li Bin of Qinghua University', 2 April 2013, http://scrapweapons.com/2013/04/02/scrap-interview-with-chinese-arms-control-expert-professor-li-bin-of-qinghua-university/.

21 Chinese strategists are obviously worried about the possibility that the US will develop new types of weapons against which they do not have adequate defences, but at this point they may hope that these will be sidetracked by technical problems and budgetary constraints. Expressions of concern over the allegedly destabilising effects of possible new offensive and defensive systems may be genuine, but they are also clearly intended to influence the debate in the US over which programmes to fund.

22 Discussion of a treaty for the 'Prevention of an Arms Race in Outer Space' has been under way at the UN Disarmament Commission since the early 1980s. In 2008, Russia and China put forward a proposal for a 'Treaty on the Placement of Weapons in Outer Space, the Threat or Use of Force Against Outer Space Objects'. See Federation of American Scientists, 'Prevention of an Arms Race in Outer Space', www.fas.org/programs/ssp/nukes/ArmsControl_NEW/nonproliferation/NFZ/

NP-NFZ-PAROS.html. For an early formulation of the arguments for a space code of conduct, see Michael Krepon, 'A Code of Conduct for Responsible Space-Faring Nations', New Delhi, November 2007, http://indianstrategicknowledgeonline.com/web/space_sec_session_1_Mr%20Michael%20Krepon.pdf.

23 Despite this, and after lengthy internal deliberations, in 2012, the Obama administration decided to go forward with a proposal for a space code of conduct. See Hillary Rodham Clinton, 'International Code of Conduct for Outer Space Activities', US Department of State, 17 January 2012, http://www.state.gov/secretary/20092013clinton/rm/2012/01/180969.htm.

24 For discussions of the potential and limitations of broad-based agreements, see James A. Lewis, 'Multilateral Agreements to Constrain Cyberconflict', Arms Control Today, June 2010, http://www.armscontrol.org/act/2010_06/lewis; Jack Goldsmith, 'Cybersecurity Treaties: A Skeptical View', in Peter Berkowitz (ed.), Future Challenges in National Security and Law (Stanford, CA: Hoover Institution Press, 2010).

25 See, for example, Kenneth Lieberthal and Peter W. Singer, Cybersecurity and US-China Relations (Washington DC: Brookings Institution, February 2012), pp. 29–31, http://www.brookings.edu/~/media/research/files/papers/2012/2/23%20cybersecurity%20china%20us%20singer%20lieberthal/0223_cybersecurity_china_us_lieberthal_singer_pdf_english.pdf.

26 The increased emphasis on precision-guided munitions and the accompanying development of the 'Air–Land Battle' doctrine, in the late 1970s and early 1980s, were directly linked to intelligence breakthroughs. Among the most important sources of information were several well-placed spies, including Colonel Ryszard Kuklinski, a Pole with access to Warsaw Pact war plans, and Colonel Ghulam Dastagir Wardark, an officer in the Afghan Army who had studied at the Voroshilov General Staff Academy. See Gordon S. Barrass, 'The Renaissance in American Strategy and the Ending of the Great Cold War', Military Review, January–February 2010, pp. 101–10. The development of the so-called 'maritime strategy', in which the US Navy reinforced the Soviet Union's inclinations to invest heavily in coastal defences by threatening to attack Soviet ballistic-missile submarines in their bastions, also hinged on intelligence breakthroughs. See Christopher A. Ford and David A. Rosenberg, 'The Naval Intelligence Underpinnings of Reagan's Maritime Strategy', Journal of Strategic Studies, vol. 28, no. 2, April 2005, pp. 379–409.

INDEX

Adelphi books are published eight times a year by Routledge Journals, an imprint of Taylor & Francis, 4 Park Square, Milton Park, Abingdon, Oxfordshire OX14 4RN, UK.

A subscription to the institution print edition, ISSN 1944-5571, includes free access for any number of concurrent users across a local area network to the online edition, ISSN 1944-558X. Taylor & Francis has a flexible approach to subscriptions enabling us to match individual libraries' requirements. This journal is available via a traditional institutional subscription (either print with free online access, or online-only at a discount) or as part of the Strategic, Defence and Security Studies subject package or Strategic, Defence and Security Studies full text package. For more information on our sales packages please visit www.tandfonline.com/librarians_pricinginfo_journals.

2014 Annual Adelphi Subscription Rates			
Institution	£585	$1,028 USD	€865
Individual	£207	$353 USD	€282
Online only	£512	$899 USD	€758

Dollar rates apply to subscribers outside Europe. Euro rates apply to all subscribers in Europe except the UK and the Republic of Ireland where the pound sterling price applies. All subscriptions are payable in advance and all rates include postage. Journals are sent by air to the USA, Canada, Mexico, India, Japan and Australasia. Subscriptions are entered on an annual basis, i.e. January to December. Payment may be made by sterling cheque, dollar cheque, international money order, National Giro, or credit card (Amex, Visa, Mastercard).

For a complete and up-to-date guide to Taylor & Francis journals and books publishing programmes, and details of advertising in our journals, visit our website: **http://www.tandfonline.com.**

Ordering information:
USA/Canada: Taylor & Francis Inc., Journals Department, 325 Chestnut Street, 8th Floor, Philadelphia, PA 19106, USA. **UK/Europe/Rest of World:** Routledge Journals, T&F Customer Services, T&F Informa UK Ltd., Sheepen Place, Colchester, Essex, CO3 3LP, UK.

Advertising enquiries to:
USA/Canada: The Advertising Manager, Taylor & Francis Inc., 325 Chestnut Street, 8th Floor, Philadelphia, PA 19106, USA. Tel: +1 (800) 354 1420. Fax: +1 (215) 625 2940. **UK/Europe/Rest of World**: The Advertising Manager, Routledge Journals, Taylor & Francis, 4 Park Square, Milton Park, Abingdon, Oxfordshire OX14 4RN, UK. Tel: +44 (0) 20 7017 6000. Fax: +44 (0) 20 7017 6336.